Welcome to ZickZack neu!

You are continuing on a course that will take you through German-speaking countries throughout the world and will help you to understand and enjoy using German yourself. ● ● ●   For much of the time you will be working on activities with guidance from your teacher, but at the end of each chapter there is a section called **sb** *Selbstbedienung* , where you'll be able to choose for yourself activities at different levels. ● ● ●   If you want to take your time and check that you've understood, choose GOLD activities.   If you're ready to try out what you've already learned, choose ROT activities.   If you want to stretch yourself still further, then the SCHWARZ activities are for you.   For all three types of activity, you can ask your teacher for answer sheets so that you can check how you're getting on. ● ● ●   At the back of the book you can look up words or phrases that you've forgotten or don't understand and find extra help with grammar. You'll find English translations of the **sb** *Selbstbedienung* instructions, too.

Viel Spaß und mach's gut!

ZICKZACK neu

2

with new German spellings

Paul Rogers, Lawrence Briggs, Bryan Goodman-Stephens

First published in 1994 by:
Thomas Nelson and Sons Ltd

New German spelling edition in 2002 by:
Nelson Thornes Ltd
Delta Place
27 Bath Road
CHELTENHAM
GL53 7TH
United Kingdom

05 / 10 9 8 7 6 5 4 3 2

A catalogue record for this book is available from the British Library

ISBN 0 7487 6701 0

Illustrations by Clinton Banbury, Judy Byford, Finbar Hawkins, Helen Holroyd,
Louise Jackson, Jeremy Long, Lotty, Jo Moore, Julian Mosedale, Jude Wisdom,
Rosemary Woods

Photography by David Simson, Diane Collett, Alastair Jones, Mike Spencer,
Janet Walker

Printed and bound in China by Midas Printing International Ltd.

Acknowledgements

The authors and publisher acknowledge the following for granting permission
to reproduce copyright material:

Osnabrück – Marketing und Tourismus GmbH

Every effort has been made to trace the copyright holders of extracts
reprinted in this book. We apologise for any inadvertent omission, which
can be rectified in a subsequent reprint.

Lernziel 1
Was gibt es hier zu sehen?

📹 Meine Stadt

Sieh dir die Bilder, den Text und die Landkarte an und hör gut zu.
Fünf Jugendliche sprechen über ihre Stadt oder ihr Dorf.
Wie heißt jeder Wohnort auf der Karte?

Beispiel
A *Osnabrück*

1 Tulai

> Ich wohne in Osnabrück – das ist eine Stadt in Nordwestdeutschland. Für Touristen gibt es hier viel zu sehen ... den Dom, das Rathaus ..., und wir haben auch ein Schloss. Osnabrück ist eine alte Stadt ... der Dom ist sehr alt ... wir haben eine Mauer rund um die Stadt. Das Stadtzentrum ist aber modern, und die Stadthalle ist auch modern. Hier gibt es manchmal Popkonzerte.

Thomas

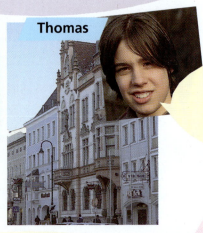

2

> Ich wohne in Braunau. Das ist eine Stadt in Österreich – im Norden an der Grenze mit Deutschland. Es gibt hier ein schönes Jugendzentrum und ein Kino. Es gibt auch ein Hallenbad, eine Sporthalle und einen Sportplatz. Es gibt viel für junge Leute, finde ich.

> Ich wohne in Passau in Südostdeutschland. Die Stadt ist ganz gut für junge Leute. Wir haben Kinos, und es gibt auch ein Jugendzentrum, Squash- und Tennishallen, ein Schwimmbad, Diskos, Cafés, alles. Ich wohne ganz gern hier.

3

Peter

> Ich wohne in Horn. Das ist ein Dorf in der Schweiz. Es gibt nichts da! Absolut nichts. Es ist stinklangweilig! Aber Zürich ist ganz in der Nähe. Da gibt's alles: Diskos, Kinos, Schwimmbäder, Tennishallen, ein großes Fußballstadion, alles.

Susi

4

Stefanie

5

> Ich wohne in Krempe. Das ist eine kleine Stadt in Norddeutschland, in der Nähe von Kiel. Es gibt nicht viel für junge Leute. Es gibt eine große Sporthalle, aber das ist alles. Wir haben keine Disko und kein Jugendzentrum. Nichts. Im Winter kann man auf dem See vor der Schule Schlittschuh laufen.

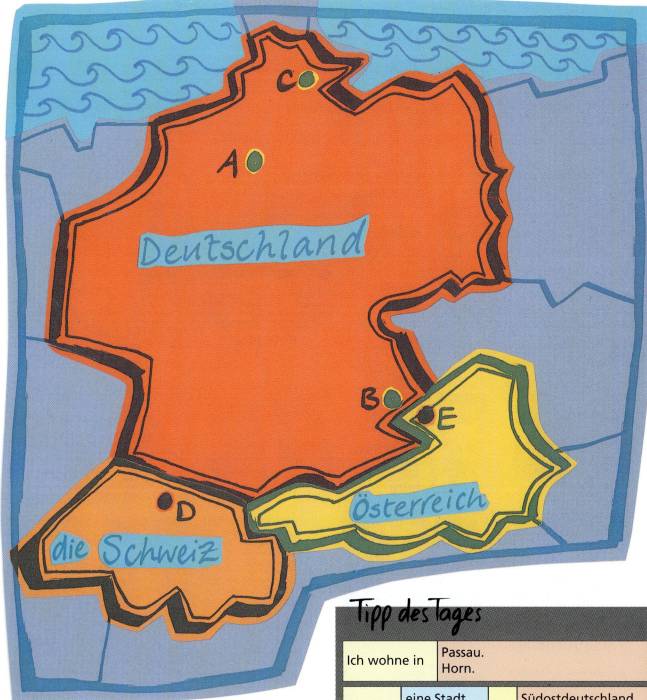

Tipp des Tages

Ich wohne in	Passau. Horn.		

Das ist	eine Stadt ein Dorf	in	Südostdeutschland. der Schweiz.

Was gibt es (hier) zu sehen?			
Gibt es (?) Es gibt	hier	einen	Dom. Campingplatz.
		eine	Stadthalle. Disko.
		ein	Schloss. Stadion.

Richtig oder falsch?

1 Die Disko in Krempe ist toll.
2 Susi wohnt gern in ihrer Stadt.
3 Für Jugendliche ist es absolut fantastisch in Horn.
4 Das Stadtzentrum in Osnabrück ist sehr alt.
5 In Passau kann man schwimmen und Tennis spielen.

Partnerarbeit. Stadtspiel

Sieh dir diese Städte und diese Bilder an.
Was gibt es in diesen Städten?
A wählt eine Stadt. B stellt Fragen. A antwortet mit ‚ja' oder ‚nein'.

Beispiel

A – Bist du fertig?
B – Ja.
A – Gibt es ein Schloss?
B – Nein.
A – Gibt es einen Bahnhof?
B – Ja.

A – Gibt es ein Kino?
B – Ja.
A – Gibt es ein Schwimmbad?
B – Nein.
A – Das ist Schönstadt.
B – Richtig.

Schlüssel
Gibt es …?

einen Dom

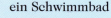
einen Bahnhof

einen Campingplatz

eine Stadthalle

ein Kino

ein Schwimmbad

ein Rathaus

ein Stadion

ein Verkehrsamt

ein Schloss

Schönstadt

Badstein

Rosendorf

Weißdorf

Sachsburg

Waldheim

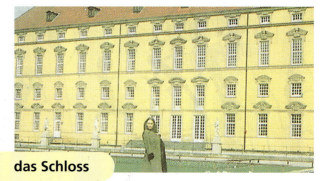

der Dom

das Schloss

Stadtrundfahrt

Diese Touristen besuchen Osnabrück und machen eine Stadtrundfahrt.
Hör gut zu.
Was sagt der Mann mit dem Mikrofon?
Wo ist das?
Links ,
rechts ➡️
oder geradeaus ⬆️ ?

Beispiel
Der Dom ist links.

Guten Morgen, meine Damen und Herren. Mein Name ist Weismann. Herzlich willkommen in Osnabrück. Wir machen jetzt eine Stadtrundfahrt.

die Stadthalle

Im Verkehrsamt

Sieh dir die Bilder an und hör gut zu.
Was bekommt die Touristin?

– Guten Tag. Was für Informationsmaterial
haben Sie über die Stadt?
– Wir haben einen Stadtplan. Wir haben auch
Broschüren, Poster, Hotellisten und sogar
auch Bücher.
– Also, ich möchte einen Stadtplan, eine
Broschüre und eine Hotelliste.
– Ja, hier, bitte schön.

– Haben Sie auch Prospekte?
– Ja, über Restaurants, Konzerte und
Ausflüge. Hier, bitte schön.
– Danke. Was kostet das, bitte?
– Gar nichts. Das ist alles kostenlos.
– Oh, schön. Vielen Dank.
– Bitte schön. Auf Wiedersehen.
– Auf Wiedersehen.

Partnerarbeit

Jetzt bist du dran Was bekommst du?
Erfinde Dialoge.

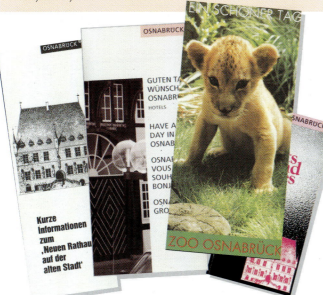

das Rathaus

die Stadtmauer

die Altstadt

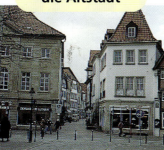

die Stadtmitte

Tipp des Tages

Der Dom Die Stadthalle Das Schloss	ist	links. rechts. geradeaus.

Haben Sie ...? Ich möchte	einen	Stadtplan. Prospekt über Konzerte. Prospekt über Ausflüge.
	eine	Broschüre. Hotelliste.
	ein	Poster.
		Bücher über die Stadt.

Was kann man hier machen?		

Man kann	den Dom das Schloss	besichtigen.
	den Zoo besuchen.	
	schwimmen gehen.	

Das interessiert mich nicht.
Nein, lieber nicht.
Oh nein!
Toll!
Prima!
Gute Idee.

Lernziel 2

Wie findest du deine Stadt?

🔊 Wie findest du Osnabrück?

Hör gut zu und sieh dir den Text an. Diese Jugendlichen sprechen über ihre Wohnorte. Was sagen sie über Osnabrück? Und über Krempe? Mach eine Tabelle.

Beispiel

	positiv	negativ
Osnabrück	Die Stadt ist ganz schön.	Es gibt zu viele Autos.

Osnabrück

Es gibt zu viele Autos.

Ich finde Osnabrück schmutzig. Es gibt zu viel Rauch.

Es ist ganz ruhig in der Fußgängerzone.

Die Stadt ist ganz schön.

Es gibt nicht genug Jobs für junge Leute hier.

Krempe

Ich wohne gern hier.

Die Stadt ist sehr sauber.

Es gibt keine Diskos und kein Jugendzentrum.

Viel zu klein.

Hier ist gar nichts los!

Braunau

Fantastisch.

Braunau gefällt mir gut.

Es gibt zu viele Touristen.

Schön, ruhig und sauber.

Ich wohne ganz gern in Braunau.

Schön, oder ...?

Sieh dir die Bilder an.
Wie findest du diese Städte und Dörfer?
Schön? Schmutzig? Ruhig?

Beispiel
Ich finde Schornsteinstadt schmutzig.

Sehenswertstadt

Schornsteinstadt

Lebendigstadt

Stadtammeer

Nichtviellos

Hübschdorf

Und wie findest du deine Stadt/dein Dorf?

Tipp des Tages

Wie findest du	deine Stadt?			Es gibt	zu viele Touristen.
	dein Dorf?				zu viele Autos.
Ich wohne gern hier.					zu viel Rauch.
Die Stadt	ist	ganz	schön.		nicht genug Jobs.
			ruhig.		keine Diskos.
			schmutzig.		kein Jugendzentrum.
			sauber.	Hier ist gar nichts los!	
		viel zu klein.			

 **Selbstbedienung**

Lernziel 1

 Straßenschilder

*Sieh dir die Straßenschilder an,
und lies die Sätze. Ist das richtig
oder falsch?*

1 Die Stadthalle ist links.
2 Der Dom ist rechts.
3 Das Stadion ist geradeaus.
4 Das Museum ist 300 Meter rechts.
5 Das Schloss ist geradeaus.

Lernziel 1

 Und deine Stadt?

*Lies den Brief und beantworte
die Fragen.*

> Minden, den 11. Oktober
> Lieber Tom!
> Vielen Dank für deinen Brief. Du
> hast mich gefragt: „Was gibt es in
> deiner Stadt zu sehen?" Also —
> ich lege dir ein paar Fotos bei.
> Es gibt den Dom in der Stadtmitte
> und natürlich das Rathaus. Wir
> haben auch eine moderne
> Stadthalle. Dort gibt es manchmal
> Popkonzerte. Letzten Samstag
> war Evi Bamm da. Toll!
> Das Jugendzentrum ist ganz
> modern. Das Stadion ist schön
> und der Fluss auch.
> Und deine Stadt — was gibt es
> dort zu sehen? Habt ihr auch ein
> Stadion und eine Stadthalle?
> Schreib bald wieder,
>   dein Andreas

1 Was war Toms Frage?
2 Was gibt es in der Stadtmitte von Minden?
3 Was gibt es manchmal in der Stadthalle?
4 Wie ist das Jugendzentrum?
5 Was findet Andreas schön?

Lernziel 1

 **Lieber Andreas!**

*Schreib den Brief – ersetz die
Bilder mit den passenden Wörtern.*

> Sale, den 22 Oktober
>
> Lieber Andreas!
>
> Leider habe ich keine Fotos von meiner Stadt,
>
> aber ich beschreibe dir alles!
>
> Wir haben und .
>
> Es gibt auch , und .
>
> Wir haben und zwei .
>
> ist in der Stadtmitte. Es gibt
>
> leider kein .
>
> Schreib bald wieder,
>
>   dein Tom

Lernziel 1

  Was kann man hier machen?

Was sagt der Tourist im Verkehrsamt?

Beispiel

Lernziel 2

  Halb und halb

Wie sind die Sätze richtig?

Beispiel
1C

1 Hier ist gar	**A** mir gut hier.
2 Es gefällt	**B** gern in Braunau.
3 Ich wohne nicht	**C** nichts los!
4 Es gibt zu viel	**D** genug Jugendzentren.
5 Es gibt nicht	**E** dein Dorf?
6 Wie findest du	**F** Rauch und zu viele Autos.
7 Die Stadt ist	**G** ganz ruhig und sauber.

Lernziel 2

  Meine Stadt

Mach ein Poster von deiner Stadt.

Beispiel

Bildvokabeln In der Stadt

1 Asking questions

Was gibt es (hier) zu sehen?				What is there to see (here)?		
Gibt es	(hier)	einen eine ein	Campingplatz? Stadthalle? Verkehrsamt?	Is there	a campsite a concert hall a tourist office	(here)?
Haben Sie		einen eine ein	Stadtplan? Broschüre? Poster?	Have you got	a street map? a brochure? a poster?	
Wie findest du		deine dein	Stadt? Dorf?	What do you think of	your town? your village?	

2 Saying what there is in town

Es gibt	(hier)	einen Dom. eine Stadthalle. ein Schloss.	There's	a cathedral a concert hall a castle	(here).

3 Saying where places are

Der Dom Die Stadthalle Das Schloss	ist	links. rechts. geradeaus.	The cathedral The concert hall The castle	is	on the left. on the right. straight ahead.

4 Asking for items in a tourist office

Ich möchte	einen	Stadtplan.
		Prospekt über
		   Konzerte/Ausflüge.
			I would like	a town plan.
				a leaflet about
				   concerts/outings.

	eine	Broschüre Hotelliste.		a brochure. a list of hotels.
	ein	Poster.		a poster.
		Bücher über die Stadt.		books about the town.

5 Commenting on a town or village

Ich wohne gern hier.				I like living here.		
Die Stadt	ist	ganz	schön. ruhig. schmutzig. sauber.	The town is	quite	nice. quiet. dirty. clean.
		viel zu klein.				much too small.
	gefällt mir gut.			I like the town.		

Es gibt	zu viele Touristen. zu viele Autos. nicht genug Jobs. keine Diskos. zu viel Rauch. kein Jugendzentrum.	There are	too many tourists. too many cars. not enough jobs. no discos.
		There is	too much smoke. no youth centre.
Hier ist gar nichts los!		It's completely dead here!	
Der Dom/Das Schloss interessiert mich nicht.		I'm not interested in the cathedral/castle.	

auf einen Blick

Lernziel 1
Wo ist hier die Post?

 **Stadtplan**

Sieh dir den Plan an und hör gut zu.
Ist das richtig oder falsch?

Beispiel
1 *falsch*

1 – Wo ist hier das Krankenhaus?
– Hier, vier A, in der Martinistraße.

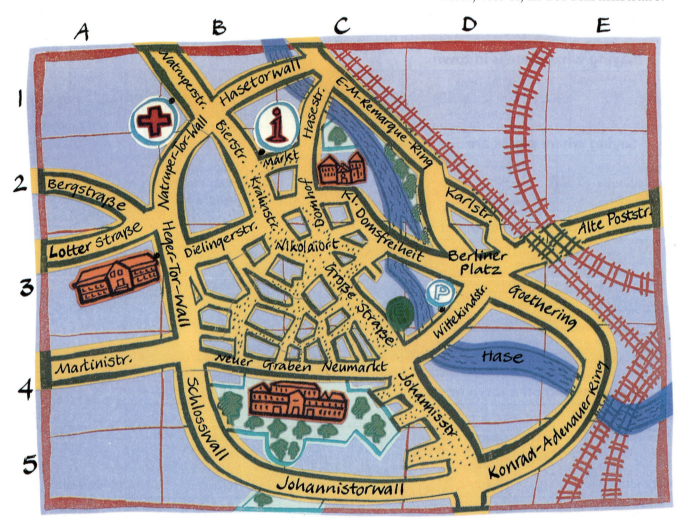

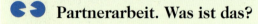

Partnerarbeit. Was ist das?

Stell und beantworte Fragen.

Beispiel

A – Drei D – in der Wittekindstraße.
Was ist das?
B – (Das ist) der Parkplatz.
A – Richtig. Jetzt bist du dran.
B – Eins B – in der ...

Schlüssel
Museum
Schloss
Dom
Parkplatz
Verkehrsamt
Fußgängerzone
Krankenhaus

Wer spricht?

Was passt wozu?

Beispiel

1 *G*

Jetzt bist du dran. Zeichne andere Bilder mit Text.

Wie ist es richtig?

Drei Personen machen es falsch. Welche Person macht es richtig?

Tipp des Tages

	die	nächste	Post? Bank?
Entschuldigung. Wo ist hier	der		Bahnhof? Dom?
	die		Fußgängerzone
	das		Verkehrsamt? Krankenhaus?
Der Parkplatz ist in der Wittekindstraße.			

Partnerarbeit.
Ist hier ein Kino in der Nähe?

Stell und beantworte Fragen.
Ersetz die Wörter in Grün.

Beispiel
A – *Ist hier* **ein Kino** *in der Nähe?*
B – *Ja.* **In der Krahnstraße**, *hier.*

◆Schlüssel◆
Kino
Bank
Restaurant
Schwimmbad
Park
Sporthalle
Campingplatz

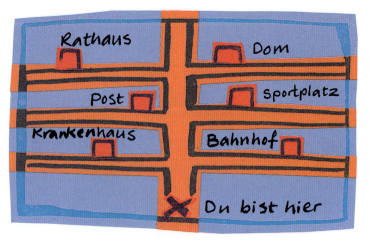

Partnerarbeit. Erste Straße links

Sieh dir den Stadtplan an und mach Dialoge.

Beispiel
A – *Entschuldigung. Wo ist der Bahnhof?*
B – *Die erste Straße rechts.*

Tipp des Tages

Ist hier	ein	Sportplatz Kino	in der Nähe?
	eine	Bank	

Wo ist die Post, bitte?			

Die	erste zweite dritte	Straße	links. rechts.

Geradeaus.		

Das ist auf der	linken rechten	Seite.

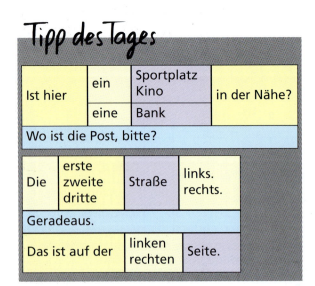

Lernziel 2
Wo ist das genau?

1
– Entschuldigung. Ich suche das Haus Walhalla.
– Wo ist das, bitte?
– In der Bierstraße.

A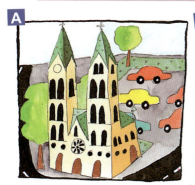

B

C

D

E

F

G

H

I

J

Tipp des Tages

Wo ist das	Auto? Verkehrsamt?		
Im Parkhaus.			
In der Poststraße.			
Hinter	dem		Dom. Rathaus.
Vor	der		Stadthalle. Kirche.
Am Marktplatz.			
An der Bushaltestelle.			
Da drüben.			

 Partnerarbeit

Beispiel
A – *Bild A – wo ist der Parkplatz?*
B – *Hinter dem Dom.*

am
an der

im
in der

vor dem
vor der

hinter dem
hinter der

Ist das weit von hier?

Hör gut zu. Wohin gehen die Personen?
Zum Bahnhof? Zur Post?
Wie weit ist das?

Beispiel
1 *Post (10 Minuten mit dem Bus)*

Tipp des Tages

Ich suche	den Bahnhof.
	die Post.
	das Verkehrsamt.

Ist das weit von hier?

Hundert Zweihundert	Meter.
Ein Kilometer.	

Fünf Zehn	Minuten	zu Fuß. mit dem Bus.

Partnerarbeit

Mach Dialoge.

Beispiel
A – *Ich suche die Post.*
   Ist das weit von hier?
B – *Ja, zehn Minuten mit dem Bus.*
A – *Danke. Auf Wiedersehen.*

Wo ist das Schwimmbad?

Hör zu und lies den Text.

Entschuldigen Sie, bitte. Ich suche das Schwimmbad. Ist es weit von hier?

Entschuldigung. Wo ist hier das Schwimmbad?

Ich kann dir leider nicht helfen, ich bin hier fremd.

Keine Ahnung. Ich wohne nicht hier.

Entschuldigung. Wo geht's denn hier zum Schwimmbad?

Das Schwimmbad? Ich weiß nicht.

Zum Schwimmbad, bitte?

Du gehst hier geradeaus und dann links, nein rechts, und dann ist das Schwimmbad auf der rechten Seite. Nein, das stimmt nicht ... du gehst hier links ...

Danke.

Das Schwimmbad?

Zum Schwimmbad?

Das ist weit. Am besten fährst du mit dem Bus, Nummer 12 oder 40.

Ja.

Ach nein!

ÖFFNUNGSZEITEN	
Montag	••••• GESCHLOSSEN
Dienstag	••••• 9.00 - 21.00
Mittwoch	••••• 7.00 - 21.00
Donnerstag	••••• 7.00 - 23.00
Freitag	••••• 7.00 - 21.00
Samstag	••••• 9.00 - 19.00
Sonntag	••••• 9.00 - 16.00

GESCHLOSSEN

sb ▶ Selbstbedienung

Lernziel 1

 Spiegelbilder

Hier siehst du alles wie im Spiegel.
Wie ist das richtig? Schreib es auf.

> Entschuldigung.
> Wo ist hier...?

Beispiel
1 *die POST*

Lernziel 1

 Wo ist das Museum?

Schreib die Dialoge auf.

Beispiel
1 – Wo ist das Museum?
  – Hier rechts.

Lernziel 1

 Wo ist hier das nächste Kino?

Sieh dir den Stadtplan an.
Wo ist das Kino?

Hier geradeaus, dann die zweite Straße
links. Dann die zweite Straße rechts.
Dann die erste Straße rechts, dann
links ... dann gleich rechts ... dann
gleich links. Dann geradeaus, dann die
zweite Straße rechts. Dann die dritte
Straße rechts, dann wieder die dritte
Straße rechts. Hier geradeaus und
dann die erste Straße rechts. Dann
kommst du schließlich zum Kino.

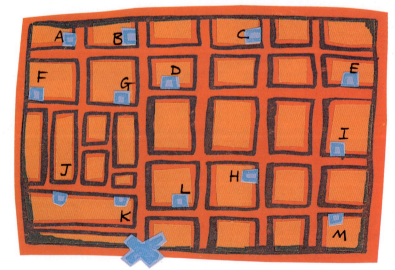

Selbstbedienung sb

Lernziel 2

Lernziel 2

 Im Restaurant

Lies den Text und sieh dir die Tische im Restaurant an. Wo sitzen die Personen?

Beispiel
1 *Tisch H*

1 Ich sitze am Tisch vor der Damentoilette.
2 Ich sitze am Tisch hinten rechts vor der Pflanze.
3 Ich sitze am Tisch vor dem Eingang.
4 Ich sitze am Tisch hinten links hinter der Pflanze.
5 Ich sitze links am Fenster.
6 Ich sitze am Tisch vor dem Ausgang.
7 Ich sitze rechts am Fenster.
8 Ich sitze am Tisch rechts vor der Herrentoilette.

Lernziel 2

 Wie weit ist das Krankenhaus von hier?

Beispiel
Das Krankenhaus ist ein Kilometer von hier.

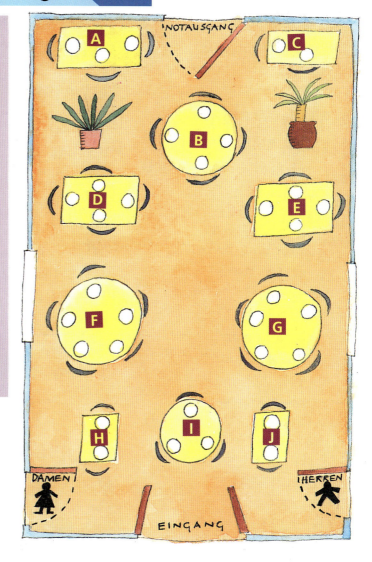

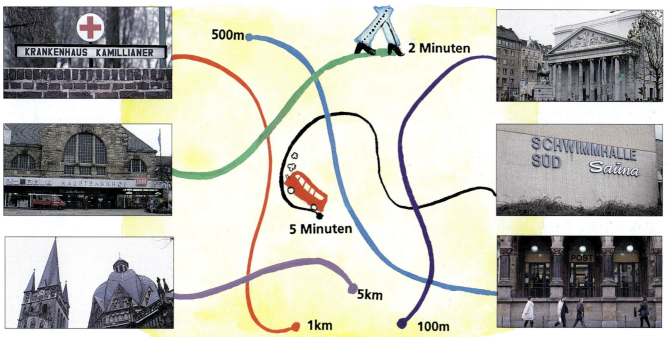

Touristen

Hör zu und sing mit.

Überall Touristen
In dieser feinen Stadt.
Leider scheint's, dass keiner
Einen Stadtplan hat.
Alle hundert Meter
Hält mich einer an.
Es gibt nur eine Antwort,
Die ich geben kann:

„Erste links, zweite rechts,
Dann geradeaus!"
Wenn ich das nicht sage,
Komm' ich nie nach Haus'!

Im Winter wie im Sommer,
Touristen überall.
Wohin sie gehen wollen,
Das ist mir egal.
„Wo ist das Museum?"
„Ist hier eine Bank?"
Ich gebe meine Antwort,
Sie sagen: „Vielen Dank!"

Refrain

Sie fragen: „Welche Straße?"
Sie fragen: „Ist es weit?"
Ich könnt' es ihnen sagen,
Doch hab' ich keine Zeit.
„Ist es in der Nähe?"
„Nehme ich den Bus?"
Du kennst ja schon
die Antwort,
Die ich geben muss:

Refrain

Ja, und dann an der Haltestelle links. Ich wohne in der Neustraße.

Geradeaus, sagst du?

Ja, danke. Tschüss!

Tschüss dann.

Mensch! Was ich alles für mein Image mache!

1 Asking questions

Entschuldigung. Wo ist hier	die	nächste	Post? Bank?	Excuse me. Where is	the	nearest	post office? bank?
	der	Bahnhof? Dom?				station? cathedral?	
	die	Fußgängerzone?				pedestrian precinct?	
	das	Verkehrsamt? Krankenhaus?				tourist info. office? hospital?	

Ist hier	ein	Sportplatz Kino	in der Nähe?	Is there	a	sports ground cinema	near here?
	eine	Bank				bank	

Ich suche	den Bahnhof. die Post. das Verkehrsamt.	I'm looking for	the station. the post office. the tourist information office.
Ist das weit von hier?		Is it far from here?

2 Saying where places are

Die	erste zweite dritte	Straße	links. rechts.	The	first second third	street	on the left. on the right.
Geradeaus.				Straight ahead.			
Das ist auf der	linken rechten	Seite.		It's on the	left hand side. right hand side.		

Im Parkhaus.		In the multi-storey car park.	
In der Poststraße.		In Poststraße.	
Hinter	dem	Dom. Rathaus.	Behind		cathedral. town hall.
Vor	der	Stadthalle. Kirche.	In front of	the	concert hall. church.
Am Marktplatz.		In the market place.	
An der Bushaltestelle.		At the bus stop.	
Da drüben.		Over there.	

3 Saying how far away places are

Hundert Zweihundert	Meter.	One hundred Two hundred	metres.
Ein Kilometer.		One kilometre.	

Fünf Zehn	Minuten	zu Fuß. mit dem Bus.	Five Ten	minutes	on foot. by bus.

Partnerarbeit.
Welches Geschäft ist das?

Stell und beantworte Fragen.
Beispiel
A – Bild 5 – welches Geschäft ist das?
B – Das ist die Metzgerei.

Lernziel 1

Wo kauft man das?

die Bäckerei

das Sportgeschäft

die Drogerie

die Buchhandlung

die Metzgerei

der Markt

die Apotheke

das Kleidergeschäft

die Konditorei

das Schuhgeschäft

🎞 Was kann man hier kaufen?

Sieh dir die Bilder an und hör gut zu.
Was kann man hier kaufen?
Beispiel
1 C *(Brot und Brötchen)*

A — Zahnpasta, Filme, Seife

B — Bücher und Zeitschriften

C — Brot und Brötchen

D — Bananen und Äpfel

E — Fleisch, Wurst, Schinken

F — Fußbälle und Turnschuhe

G — Kuchen und Kekse

H — Schuhe und Sandalen

I — Tabletten und Hustenbonbons

J — Jeans, Pullover, T-Shirts

🔶🔶 Partnerarbeit.
Am Markt, oder?

A – Wo kauft man Brot?
B – In der Bäckerei. Wo kauft man Wurst?
A – In der Metzgerei. Und Schuhe?
B – Im Schuhgeschäft. Und Bananen?
A – Am Markt.

Tipp des Tages

Wo kauft man das?

Man kauft	Brot	in der	Bäckerei.
	Zahnpasta		Drogerie.
	Kuchen		Konditorei.
	Fleisch		Metzgerei.
	Tabletten		Apotheke.
	Bücher		Buchhandlung.
	Schuhe		Schuhgeschäft.
	Kleider	im	Kleidergeschäft.
	Sportartikel		Sportgeschäft.
	Äpfel	am	Markt.

Ralf der Räuber

Ralf der Räuber geht einkaufen.
Er hat kein Geld, aber eine Pistole.
Hör zu und lies den Text.

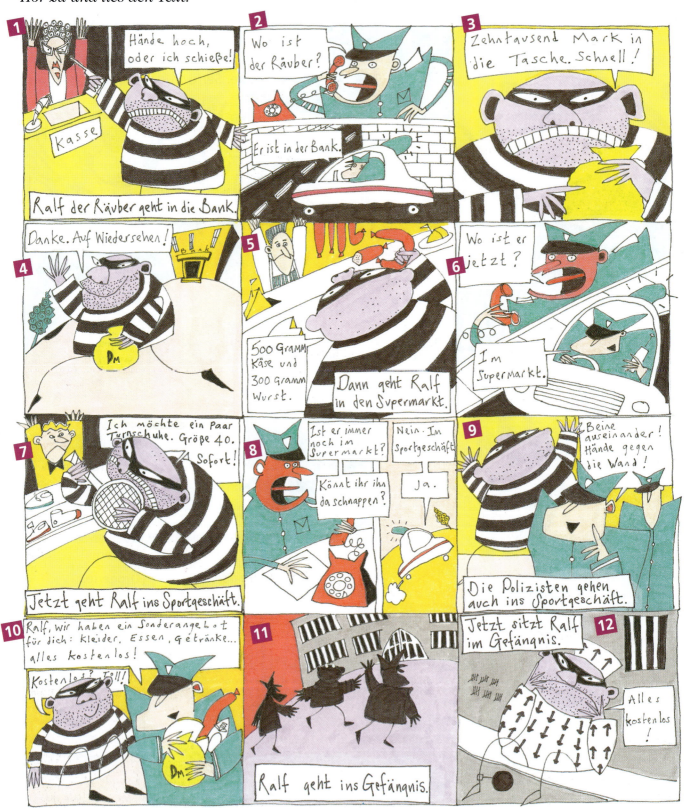

Jörgs Einkaufsliste

Lies den Dialog zwischen Jörg und seiner Mutter und ersetz die Bilder. Schreib ‚in den', ‚in die' oder ‚auf den' und dann den Geschäftsnamen.

Beispiel
A *in die Bäckerei*

Frau Jührend

Jörg, gehst du bitte einkaufen?

Jörg

Ja, gerne. Was soll ich denn holen?

Zuerst kannst du   gehen. Kauf bitte ein Landbrot und fünf Brötchen. Geh dann und kauf 200 Gramm Leberwurst und 300 Gramm Schinken. Dann gehst du und kaufst ein Pfund Tomaten.

Alles klar. Was sonst noch?

Ich habe keinen Käse und keine Kekse mehr. Geh also bitte

Wäre das alles?

Ja ... nein, warte mal! Geh auch

Warum denn das?

Ich habe Kopfschmerzen. Ich brauche Tabletten.

Gut. Am besten mache ich eine Liste.

Ja, aber mach schnell! Es wird spät!

Einkaufsliste

Schreib jetzt Jörgs Einkaufsliste.

Wo treffen sie sich vielleicht?

Sieh dir diese drei Einkaufslisten an und hör zu.
Wem gehört jede Liste – Karin, Jörg oder Uschi?

A
Fußballschuhe
Pullover
Zeitschrift
1 Pfund Äpfel
Hustenbonbons
Seife

B
200 Gramm Käse
500 Gramm Butter
Sandalen
1 Film
1 Kilo Bananen
Aspirintabletten

C
• Zahnpasta
• TV-Zeitschrift
• Bücher
• Tennisbälle
• T-Shirt
• Schuhe

Wo treffen sich diese Leute vielleicht? Im Schuhgeschäft, oder ...?
Vorsicht! Es gibt keinen Supermarkt im Dorf!

Tipp des Tages

Ich gehe	in den	Supermarkt.	Er ist	im	Gefängnis.
	in die	Drogerie.		in der	Bank.
	ins	Schuhgeschäft.			
	auf den	Markt.			

Lernziel 2

Wie viel ist das?

Wie viel?

Sieh dir die Bilder an.

ein Liter Milch

fünfhundert Gramm Käse

Ein Kilo – das sind genau zwei Pfund

Ein Pfund Tomaten – fünfhundert Gramm

zweihundert Gramm Wurst

ein halber Liter Cola

Ein Gramm Käse - das reicht einer Maus für einen Tag

Hundert Liter Wasser - das reicht einem Kamel für eine Woche.

 Das Einkaufslied

Hör zu und sing mit.

Ich gehe gern einkaufen
Im Supermarkt.
Ich muss alles kaufen,
Was Mutti mir sagt:

3
Hundert Gramm Bierwurst,
Ein Pfund Bananen,
Ein Glas Konfitüre,
Ein Pfund Tomaten.

2
Eine Flasche Cola,
Ein Becher Jogurt,
'ne Schachtel Pralinen,
Kartoffeln und Brot.

1
Zahnpasta, Apfelsaft,
Käse und Tee,
Und wenn du noch Geld hast,
Dann eine CD.

Was kaufen die Leute im Geschäft?

Hör gut zu. Was kaufen sie?
Wie ist die richtige
Reihenfolge?
Schreib 1 bis 14 in dein Heft.
Beispiel
1 *H*

B fünf Kilo Kartoffeln

C dreihundert Gramm Käse

D eine Dose Cola

A anderthalb Kilo Käse

F eine Packung Kekse

G eine Dose Tomatensuppe

H ein Kilo Tomaten

E ein Glas Marmelade

I eine Packung Kaffee

J eine Schachtel Pralinen

K ein Marsriegel

L ein Glas Honig

M eine Flasche Apfelsaft

N ein Liter Milch

O ein Becher Margarine

P ein Stück Seife

Q eine Tube Zahnpasta

R eine Tüte Gummibärchen

Tipp des Tages

Hundert Zweihundert	Gramm		Wurst. Käse.
Ein	Pfund Kilo		Tomaten. Kartoffeln.
	Liter halber Liter		Milch. Wasser.
Das reicht	einer Person.		
	für fünf belegte Brote.		
Ein	Glas		Honig.
	Stück		Seife.
	Becher		Margarine.
	Riegel		Schokolade.
Eine	Schachtel		Pralinen.
	Tube		Zahnpasta.
	Packung		Kekse.
	Dose		Tomatensuppe.
	Flasche		Milch.
	Tüte		Gummibärchen.

Partnerarbeit. Einkaufslisten

Schreib eine Einkaufsliste und diktiere sie
deinem Partner/deiner Partnerin.
Beispiel
eine Dose Tomatensuppe
eine Packung Kaffee

Selbstbedienung

Lernziel 1

 Welches Geschäft ist das?

Schreib die Geschäfte auf.
Beispiel
1 *Das ist die Bäckerei.*

Lernziel 1

 Wo sind die Sachen?

In welcher Tasche sind diese Artikel?
In Tasche 1, 2, 3, 4 oder 5?
Beispiel
Der Käse ist in Tasche 1.

Die Cola ist rechts von der Tasche mit der Schokolade.

Der Käse ist in der blauen Tasche.

Die Wurst ist in der gelben Tasche.

Die Gummibärchen sind links von der Tasche mit der Wurst.

Die Schokolade ist in der braunen Tasche.

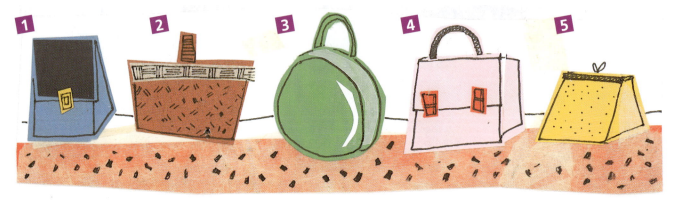

Lernziel 1

Purzelwörter

Wie ist es richtig? Und wo kauft man das?
Beispiel
1 *Buch — in der Buchhandlung*

1 CHUB

2 HAZAPANTS

3 SHUNNOBOTNBES

4 LENANDAS

5 PRUVELLO

Schreib jetzt andere Purzelwörter.

Lernziel 2

🚩 Wie viel?

Was passt am besten?
Schreib es richtig auf.

Beispiel
Ein Liter Milch

Eine Tube	Cola
Zweihundert Gramm	Milch
Ein Liter	Kaffee
Ein Becher	Zahnpasta
Fünf Kilo	Kartoffeln
Eine Tüte	Käse
Eine Packung	Gummibärchen
Eine Dose	Margarine

Lernziel 2

🚩 Im Doofimarkt!

Hier ist alles verrückt!
Zeichne verrückte Bilder!

Eine Tube Gummibärchen   Eine Tüte Cola

Lernziel 2

🚩 Meine Einkaufsliste

Sieh dir die Bilder und Wörter an und schreib eine Einkaufsliste.

Beispiel

Einkaufsliste
1 Kilo Bananen

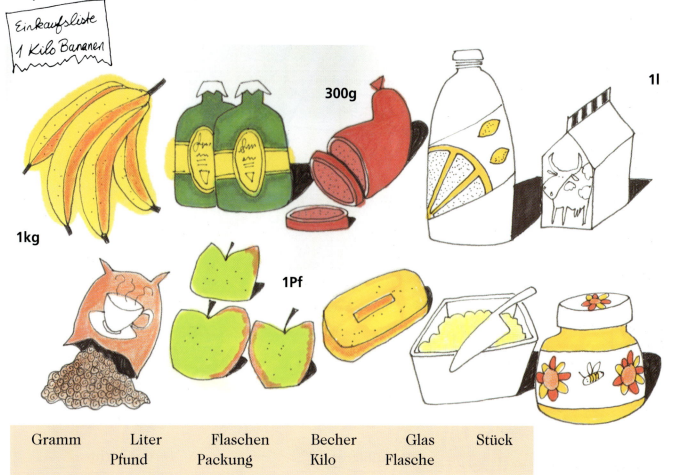

Gramm	Liter	Flaschen	Becher	Glas	Stück
	Pfund	Packung	Kilo	Flasche	

Bildvokabeln **Im Supermarkt**

Feinkost

Backwaren

Feinkost

Backwaren

Waschmittel

Obst und Gemüse

Lebensmittel

Reinigungsmittel

Alkoholische Getränke

Konserven

Milchprodukte

Haustiernahrung

Getränke

Kosmetik

Tiefkühlkost

Fertiggerichte

auf einen Blick

1 Asking questions

Wo kauft man das?	*Where do you buy that?*
Was kann man hier kaufen?	*What can you buy here?*
Wie viel ist das?	*How much is that?*

2 Saying which shop you are going to

Ich gehe	in den	Supermarkt.	I'm going	to the	*supermarket.*
	in die	Drogerie.			*chemist's.*
	ins	Schuhgeschäft.			*shoe shop.*
	auf den	Markt.			*market.*

3 Saying where you buy things

Man kauft	Brot		Bäckerei.	You buy	bread		*baker's.*
	Zahnpasta		Drogerie.		toothpaste		*chemist's.*
	Kuchen		Konditorei.		cakes	at the	*cake shop.*
	Fleisch	in der	Metzgerei.		meat		*butcher's.*
	Tabletten		Apotheke.		tablets		*pharmacy.*
	Bücher		Buchhandlung.		books		*bookshop.*
	Schuhe		Schuhgeschäft.		shoes		*shoe shop.*
	Kleider	im	Kleidergeschäft.		clothes	in the	*boutique.*
	Sportartikel		Sportgeschäft.		sportswear		*sports shop.*
	Äpfel	am	Markt.		apples	at the	*market.*

4 Weights and containers

Hundert Zweihundert	Gramm	Wurst. Käse.	One hundred Two hundred	grams of	*sausage.* *cheese.*

Ein	Pfund	Tomaten.	One	pound of	*tomatoes.*
	Kilo	Kartoffeln.		kilo of	*potatoes.*
	Liter	Milch.		litre of	*milk.*
	halber Liter	Wasser.	Half a litre of		*water.*
Anderthalb	Kilo	Bananen.	One and a half	kilos of	*bananas.*

Das reicht	einer Person.	That's enough for	*one person.*
	für fünf belegte Brote.		*five sandwiches.*

Ein	Glas	Honig.	A	jar of	*honey.*
	Stück	Seife.		bar of	*soap.*
	Becher	Margarine.		tub of	*margarine.*
	Riegel	Schokolade.		bar of	*chocolate.*
Eine	Schachtel	Pralinen.		box of	*chocolates.*
	Tube	Zahnpasta.		tube of	*toothpaste.*
	Packung	Kekse.		packet of	*biscuits.*
	Dose	Tomatensuppe.		tin of	*tomato soup.*
	Flasche	Milch.		bottle of	*milk.*
	Tüte	Gummibärchen.		bag of	*jelly babies.*

Lernziel 1
Verkehrsmittel

A B C E G

Wie kommst du dahin?

Sieh dir die Bilder an und hör gut zu.
Was passt wozu?

Beispiel
1 *C*

D

F

H

I

Wie fahren sie dahin?

Schreib diese Sätze in dein Heft und füll die Lücken aus.
Beispiel

 Ich komme *mit dem Rad* zur Schule.

2 Ich *fliege* nach New York.

3  Ich fahre _____ in die Stadt.

4 Ich komme _____ in die Stadt.

5  Ich fahre _____ zum Sportplatz.

6  Ich fahre _____ nach Harwich ... und _____ nach Hamburg.

7 Ich gehe _____ zur Disko.

8  Mein Vater bringt mich_____ zur Party.

Partnerarbeit. Wie kommst du zum Sportplatz?

Stell und beantworte Fragen.

Beispiel
A – Wie kommst du zum Sportplatz?
B – Mit dem Rad.
A – Wie kommst du zur Schule?
B – …
A – Wie kommst du nach Folkestone?
B – …

Sonntags bin ich immer müde!

Asla beschreibt, wie sie jeden Sonntag zu ihrer Großmutter kommt.
Das ist eine lange, komplizierte Reise.
Hör gut zu und lies den Text. Wie kommt sie dahin?
Wähl die richtige Antwort.

Sportplatz   Disko   Kino   Folkestone   Schule

?   ?   ?   ?   ?

> Jeden Sonntag gehe ich zu meiner Großmutter. Sie wohnt in einem Dorf auf dem Land. Ich stehe früh auf und fahre mit dem Rad zum Bahnhof. Dann fahre ich mit dem Zug nach Hamburg. In Hamburg fahre ich mit der Straßenbahn zum Busbahnhof. Dann fahre ich zwanzig Minuten mit dem Bus zu dem Dorf, wo meine Großmutter wohnt. Von der Bushaltestelle gehe ich dann fünf Minuten zu Fuß. Es ist nicht sehr weit, aber es dauert immer mehr als zwei Stunden.

A
B
C
D

Jetzt bist du dran!

Beschreib eine lange, komplizierte Reise, die du jede Woche, jeden Monat oder jedes Jahr machst.

Tipp des Tages

Wie kommst du	zum	Sportplatz? Schwimmbad?
	zur	Party? Schule? Disko?
	nach	England? Köln?

Ich fahre	mit	dem	Wagen. Bus. Zug. Rad. Mofa.
Wir fahren		der	Straßenbahn. S-Bahn. U-Bahn. Fähre.

Ich gehe Wir gehen	zu Fuß.

Ich fliege.
Wir fliegen.

Wie fährst du?

Lies das Interview.
Wie fahren die Jugendlichen?
Schreib die Tabelle in dein Heft.
Was sind die Vor- und Nachteile der Verkehrsmittel?

Am liebsten fahre ich mit dem Rad. Es gibt gute Fahrradwege in meiner Stadt, und Radfahren macht fit, ist billig und ist auch umweltfreundlich.

Karin

Ich fahre meistens mit dem Bus, denn ich wohne etwas außerhalb der Stadt. Normalerweise ist das kein Problem, aber ich muss manchmal ziemlich lange auf einen Bus warten.

Cordula

Ich habe mein eigenes Auto. Mit dem Auto kommt man viel direkter und schneller hin. Ich weiß, das ist nicht sehr umweltfreundlich und ist auch ziemlich teuer, aber es spart mir viel Zeit.

Peter

Normalerweise gehe ich zu Fuß oder fahre mit dem Rad. Ich fahre nur sehr selten mit dem Auto in der Stadt. Zu Fuß gehen ist gesund und kostet auch nichts. Es gefällt mir bloß nicht, wenn es regnet!

Lutz

Ich wohne mitten in einer Großstadt, und ich fahre entweder mit der Straßenbahn oder mit der U-Bahn. Beides ist für mich sehr praktisch.

Manchmal fahre ich mit dem Bus, aber am liebsten fahre ich mit der S-Bahn. Die fährt sehr schnell und direkt, und man muss nicht lange warten. Als Schülerin bekomme ich da auch eine Ermäßigung – das kostet dann auch nicht zu viel.

Sandra

Helene

Ich habe ein Mofa, wie alle meine Freunde. Ich finde das praktisch – es kostet nicht zu viel, macht frei und hat nur einen kleinen Benzinverbrauch.

Karl

		Vorteile	Nachteile
Beispiel	Rad	gute Fahrradwege, billig…	
	Mofa		
	Auto		
	Bus		
	S-Bahn		
	Straßenbahn		
	zu Fuß		
	U-Bahn		

Lernziel 2
Wie komme ich dahin?

 Entschuldigung ... Ich suche den Bahnhof

*Sieh dir die Bilder an und hör gut zu.
Was passt wozu?*

Beispiel
1 *E*

A

B

C

D

E

 Partnerarbeit. Der Bus nach Schenefeld kommt

Stell deinem Partner/deiner Partnerin Fragen.

Beispiel
A – Der Bus nach Schenefeld, welche Linie ist das?
B – Das ist die Linie 37.

Tipp des Tages

Wie komme ich am besten	zum	(nächsten)	Busbahnhof? Flugplatz?
	zur		U-Bahnstation? S-Bahnhaltestelle
	nach	Thesdorf?	

| Der Bus nach | Pinneberg, | welche Linie ist das? |

| Das ist die Linie | dreiundfünfzig. |

FAHRPLAN

Buslinie	Richtung
26	Wedel
37	Schenefeld
53	Pinneberg
65	Quickborn
78	Uetersen
81	Tornesch
84	Elmshorn
92	Appen

Welche Linie ist das?

Das ist ein Plan vom Münchener Verkehrsnetz.
Hör gut zu. Welche Linie ist das?

Beispiel

1 *S2*

🔵🔵 **Partnerarbeit**

Du bist am Münchener Hauptbahnhof.
Stell und beantworte Fragen.

Beispiel

A – Entschuldigung. Ich muss nach Ebersberg.
Welche Linie ist das?

B – Ebersberg ist die Linie S5.

A – Vielen Dank.

B – Nichts zu danken.

Einmal nach Pfarrkirchen, bitte

Hör zu und lies die Dialoge.

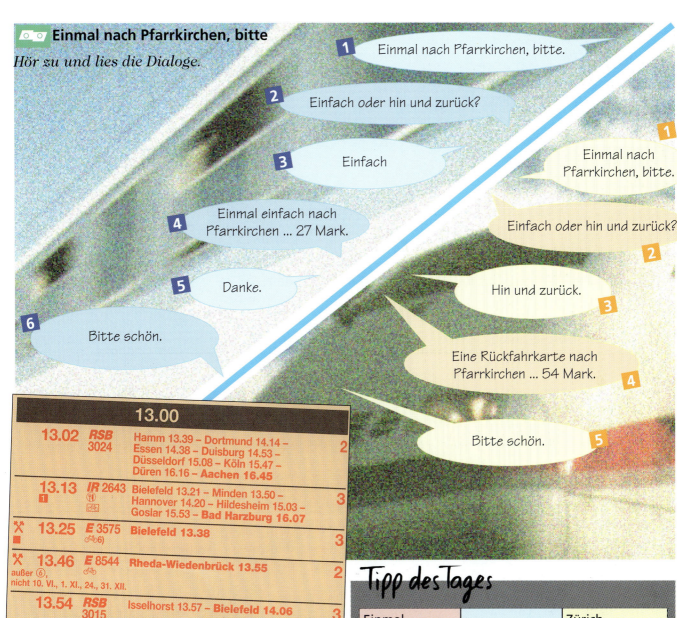

1 Einmal nach Pfarrkirchen, bitte.

2 Einfach oder hin und zurück?

3 Einfach

4 Einmal einfach nach Pfarrkirchen ... 27 Mark.

5 Danke.

6 Bitte schön.

1 Einmal nach Pfarrkirchen, bitte.

2 Einfach oder hin und zurück?

3 Hin und zurück.

4 Eine Rückfahrkarte nach Pfarrkirchen ... 54 Mark.

5 Bitte schön.

13.00

13.02	*RSB* 3024	Hamm 13.39 – Dortmund 14.14 – Essen 14.38 – Duisburg 14.53 – Düsseldorf 15.08 – Köln 15.47 – Düren 16.16 – **Aachen 16.45**	2
13.13 ☐1	*IR* 2643 ⚲	Bielefeld 13.21 – Minden 13.50 – Hannover 14.20 – Hildesheim 15.03 – Goslar 15.53 – **Bad Harzburg 16.07**	3
✗ 13.25 ■	*E* 3575 🚲6)	**Bielefeld 13.38**	3
✗ 13.46 außer ⑥, nicht 10. VI., 1. XI., 24., 31. XII.	*E* 8544 🚲	Rheda-Wiedenbrück 13.55	2
13.54	*RSB* 3015	Isselhorst 13.57 – **Bielefeld 14.06**	3

Partnerarbeit. Abfahrt

Sieh dir die Tabelle im Foto an.
Mach Dialoge.

Beispiel

A – *Entschuldigung. Wann fährt der nächste Zug nach Bielefeld?*

B – *Nach Bielefeld. Moment mal. Ja, der nächste Zug nach Bielefeld fährt um 13.13 Uhr*

A – *Von welchem Gleis?*

B – *Von Gleis 3.*

A – *Wann kommt er an?*

B – *Um 13.21 Uhr.*

Tipp des Tages

Einmal Zweimal Dreimal	nach	Zürich. Berlin. Wien.

Einfach oder hin und zurück?

Einmal nach Zürich, einfach.

Eine Rückfahrkarte nach Pfarrkirchen, bitte.

Wann	fährt der nächste Zug nach Stuttgart, bitte? kommt der Zug an?

Von welchem Gleis?

Muss ich umsteigen?

Ja, Sie müssen in Ulm umsteigen.
Nein, der Zug fährt direkt.

Selbstbedienung

Lernziel 1

 Gespräche

Lies die zwei Dialoge und wähl die richtigen Antworten in den Kästchen.

1

– Hallo, Heike!
– Hallo, Renate! Wie geht's?
– Danke, gut. Du, hör mal. Ich habe Karten für das Popkonzert am Samstag.
– Das mit Evi Bamm?
– Ja, klar!
– Oh, prima. Dann komme ich zu dir nach München ... am Samstagnachmittag. Meine Mutter bringt mich bestimmt mit dem Wagen hin.
– Kommt Andi auch mit?
– Ja, aber er kommt erst später mit der Bahn.
– O.K., tschüss. Bis Samstag.

2

– Mutti, meine Klasse plant eine Reise nach London. Darf ich mitfahren?
– Wie kommt ihr denn nach London? Mit dem Flugzeug?
– Nein, mit dem Zug nach Ostende und dann mit der Fähre nach Dover. Von da mit der Bahn weiter nach London.
– Und was kostet das?
– Nur 1 200 Mark für 14 Tage.
– Ich glaube, das ist ein bisschen teuer.

1a
Zwei Mädchen und ein Junge gehen am | Freitag / Samstag / Sonntag | zu einem Konzert.

1b
Die Popgruppe heißt | Evi Bamm. / Ede Funk. / Edelweiß.

1c
Das Popkonzert ist in | Köln. / Freiburg. / München.

1d
Ein Mädchen fährt mit dem | Wagen / Zug / Bus | dorthin.

1e
Andi fährt mit der | Bahn. / U-Bahn.

2a
Die Klasse plant eine Klassenfahrt nach | Lindau. / London. / Lohne.

2b
Sie fahren mit | der Bahn / der Fähre | nach Ostende.

2c
Dann fahren sie mit | dem Zug / dem Bus / der Fähre | weiter nach Dover.

2d
Schließlich fahren sie mit | dem Wagen / der Bahn / dem Mofa | nach London.

2e
Es kostet | DM 880,- / DM 1 200,- / DM 1 800,- | für | 4 / 14 / 40 | Tage.

Lernziel 1

 Ein Brief aus Perpignan

Lies den Brief und beantworte die Fragen.

Perpignan, den 7. Juli

Lieber Peter!
    Wir machen gerade Ferien in Frankreich. Das Wetter ist ganz toll.
    Du kommst also am 10. August zu uns nach Osnabrück? Da sind wir wieder zu Hause. Kommst du mit der Fähre und mit dem Zug direkt nach Osnabrück, oder fliegst du nach Hannover?

    Bis dann,
    dein Udo

1 Was macht Udo in Frankreich?
2 Wann kommt Peter nach Osnabrück?
3 Wie kann man nach Osnabrück fahren?
4 Wo ist der nächste Flugplatz?

Lernziel 2

 Was ist das?

Schreib es auf.

Lernziel 2

 Zweimal nach Hamburg, bitte

Schreib die Dialoge auf.

Beispiel

1 – Zweimal nach Hamburg, bitte.
  Hin und zurück.
  – Fünfundsechzig Mark, bitte.

1 2 x Hamburg
DM65,-

2 1 x Kiel
DM33,50

3 3 x Bonn
DM93,-

4 1 x Osnabrück
DM19,50

5 2 x München
DM82,-

6 1 x Köln
DM47,-

Lernziel 2

 Wann fährt der nächste Zug?

Sieh dir den Fahrplan an und beantworte die Fragen.

Beispiel

1 *Um 19.02 Uhr.*

19.02	RSB 3044	Hamm 19.39 – Dortmund 20.14 – Essen 20.38 – Duisburg 20.53 – Düsseldorf 21.08 – Köln 21.47 – Düren 22.16 – **Aachen 22.45** *Am 24., 31. XII. nur bis* **Dortmund**	2
19.13	IR 2649	Bielefeld 19.21 – Minden 19.50 – Hannover 20.20 – Braunschweig 21.06 – Magdeburg 22.02 – Halle (Saale) 23.20 – **Leipzig 23.49** *Am 24. XII. nur bis* **Magdeburg**	3
19.25 *außer ⑥, auch 1. I., nicht 24., 25., 31. XII.*	E 3583	Bielefeld 19.38 – Herford 19.56 – **Löhne 20.07** *An † und 10. VI., 1. XI. nur bis* **Herford**	3
19.41 *außer ⑥, nicht 10. VI., 1. XI., 24., 31. XII.*	E 8539 *nur 2. Kl*	Isselhorst 19.45 – **Bielefeld 19.55**	4
19.54	RSB 3033	Isselhorst 19.57 – **Bielefeld 20.06**	3

1 Wann fährt der nächste Zug nach Essen?

2 Wann kommt der E3583 in Löhne an?

3 Von welchem Gleis in Gütersloh fährt der Zug um 19.54 Uhr?

4 Wie viele Züge fahren nach Bielefeld zwischen 19.00 Uhr und 20.00 Uhr?

5 Wie lange dauert die Reise von Gütersloh nach Duisburg?

Bildvokabeln

Am Bahnhof

- der Bahnsteig
- das Bahnhofsrestaurant
- die Auskunft
- der Kiosk
- der Schalter
- das Fundbüro
- die Apotheke
- die Gepäckaufbewahrung
- Schließfächer
- der Warteraum
- der Geldwechsel
- der Fahrkartenautomat
- der Kofferkuli

Steffi

Halb zwölf!

Ich hab' den letzten Bus verpasst. Vati, ich brauch' unbedingt ein Mofa . . . alle meine Freunde haben eins.

Ein Mofa . . . ? Ich weiß, was du brauchst!

Was denn?

Einen Busfahrplan!

auf einen Blick

1 Asking questions

Wie kommst du	zur Schule?		How do you travel to	school?	
	zum Sportplatz?			the sports ground?	
	nach	England?			England?
		Köln?			Cologne?

Welche Linie ist das?	Which line is it?

Einfach?	Single?
Hin und zurück?	Return?

Wann	fährt der nächste Zug nach Stuttgart, bitte?	When does the next train to Stuttgart leave, please?
	kommt der Zug an?	When does the train arrive?
Von welchem Gleis?		From which platform?
Muss ich umsteigen?		Do I have to change trains?

2 Saying how you travel to places

Ich fahre		dem	Wagen.	I go		car.
	mit		Bus.			bus.
			Zug.		by	train.
			Rad.			bicycle.
			Mofa.			moped.
Wir fahren		der	Straßenbahn.	We go		tram.
			S-Bahn.			high speed urban railway.
			U-Bahn.			underground.
			Fähre.			ferry.

Ich gehe Wir gehen	zu Fuß.	I We	walk.

Ich fliege. Wir fliegen.		I We	fly.

3 Understanding travel details and buying tickets

Das ist die Linie fünfundzwanzig.	That's line 25.

Einmal		Zürich.	One ticket		Zurich.
Zweimal	nach	Berlin.	Two tickets	to	Berlin.
Dreimal		Wien.	Three tickets		Vienna.

Einmal nach Zürich, einfach.	One single ticket to Zurich.
Eine Rückfahrkarte nach Pfarrkirchen, bitte.	One return ticket to Pfarrkirchen, please.

Sie müssen in Ulm umsteigen.	You have to change in Ulm.
Der Zug fährt direkt.	It's a through train.

Lernziel 1

Sieht schön aus!

Wer ist das?

Welches Bild passt zu welchem Text?

Beispiel
A *Anja*

Asaf   Wiebke   Oliver   Anja   Gianni   Pepe   Maren   Petra

A Sie ist mittelgroß und schlank. Sie hat lange, glatte, blonde Haare und blaue Augen.

B Er ist groß. Er hat kurze, lockige, schwarze Haare und braune Augen.

C Sie ist mittelgroß. Sie hat kurze, braune Haare und braune Augen.

D Er ist ziemlich groß und dick. Er hat kurze, lockige, braune Haare und blaue Augen.

E Sie ist ziemlich klein. Sie hat lange, lockige, blonde Haare und grüne Augen.

F Er ist ziemlich klein. Er hat kurze, glatte, schwarze Haare und braune Augen.

G Er ist klein. Er hat lange blonde Haare und graue Augen.

H Sie ist sehr groß. Sie hat kurze, lockige, rote Haare und grüne Augen.

Tipp des Tages

Ich bin			groß. klein. schlank. dick.	Ich habe	kurze, lange, lockige, glatte,	schwarze braune blonde rote	Haare.
Er	ist	sehr					
		ziemlich		Er Sie	hat	blaue grüne braune graue	Augen.
Sie		mittelgroß.					

❤❤ Partnerarbeit. Haarige Probleme

Wähl eine Person.
Dein(e) Partner(in) muß erraten, wer du bist.
Beispiel

A – Bist du ein Junge?	**B** – Nein.	**A** – Trägst du eine Brille?
B – Nein.	**A** – Hast du braune Haare?	**B** – Ja.
A – Hast du lange Haare?	**B** – Ja.	**A** – Bist du Kirsten?
B – Ja.	**A** – Hast du lockige Haare?	**B** – Ja. Das waren sieben
A – Hast du schwarze Haare?	**B** – Nein.	Fragen. Jetzt bist du dran.

Jürgen

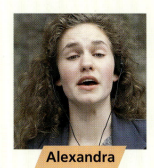
Alexandra

Kirsten

Oguz

Martin

Christian

Trudi

Connie

Renate

Tanh-Mai

Arturo

Jörg

Oliver

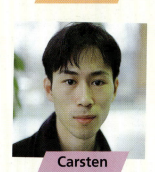
Carsten

Sabine

Bastian

Gruppenfoto

Sieh dir das Foto an, hör gut zu und lies die Sätze. Welche Person ist das?
Schreib es auf.

Beispiel
1 *(Max) = A*

1. Max trägt eine schwarze Lederjacke und eine schwarze Hose.
2. Vanessa hat blonde Haare und trägt einen roten Anorak.
3. Marie trägt einen bunten Pullover.
4. Henrike trägt eine blaue Hose zu einem blau-weiß gestreiften Pulli.
5. Tobias trägt eine schwarze Hose. Er hat kurze, blonde Haare.
6. Patrick trägt eine schwarze Jacke und ein blau-weißes Hemd. Er hat rote Haare.
7. Kerstin trägt eine grüne Jacke und braune Schuhe. Sie trägt auch eine Brille.
8. Sebastian hat kurze, braune Haare und trägt eine blau-weiß-rote Jacke.
9. Elisabeth trägt einen Anorak, eine schwarze Wolljacke und schwarze Schuhe.
10. Carlos trägt Jeans und eine blau-grüne Jacke. Er hat schwarze Haare.

bunt · schwarz · grün · rot · braun · grau · blau · weiß · gelb

Tipp des Tages

Wie sieht		er / sie	aus?
Anjas Hasans	Rock Hemd	ist	blau.
Sein Ihr	Pullover T-Shirt		rot. grün.
Seine	Jacke		weiß. schwarz.
Ihre	Schuhe	sind	grau.

Er Sie	trägt	einen blauen Pullover. eine rote Jacke. ein grünes T-Shirt. graue Schuhe.
		eine Brille

Bunte Kleider

Diese fünf Jugendlichen gehen aus.
Was tragen sie? Schreib es auf.

Beispiel
Margas Bluse ist weiß.
Nicola trägt eine gelbe Hose.

Ralf   Marga   Jochen   Gisela   Nicola

Steffi

Lernziel 2

Tolle Typen!

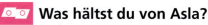 **Was hältst du von Asla?**

Wer mag Asla? Wer nicht?
Hör gut zu und lies die Texte.

Aslas Klassenlehrer

Mit Asla bin ich ganz zufrieden. Sie ist fleißig und immer pünktlich. Ich finde sie sehr sympathisch.

Sie ist ganz lieb. Sie hilft auch viel zu Hause.

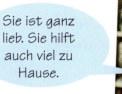 

Aslas Vater

Aslas Bruder

Die ist ziemlich O.K.

Ich kann sie nicht leiden. Die ist blöd.

Ein Mitschüler

Asla ist meine beste Freundin. Ich finde sie toll.

Anja

Ich finde sie unheimlich nett.

Eine Mitschülerin

Sie ist eine gute Tochter, aber manchmal ein bisschen unordentlich.

Aslas Mutter

Graffitimauer

Lies die Graffiti. Mach deine eigene Graffitimauer.

Partnerarbeit. Wer spricht?

Wähl eine Person auf der linken Seite und sieh dir den Schlüssel an.
Sag etwas über die Personen auf der rechten Seite.

Beispiel

A – Ja, fertig. Ich finde Markus doof, aber ich finde Petra nett. Wer bin ich?

B – Gabi.

A – Richtig. Jetzt bist du dran.

Schlüssel	
positiv	negativ
➜	〉
• nett	• fies
• sympathisch	• blöd
• toll	• doof
• O.K.	• nicht nett

Sag mir jemand, wer sie war

Hör zu und sing mit.

Ich habe sie zuerst im Park gesehen,
Hat sie mich gesehen? Das weiß ich nicht.
Ich weiß nicht, wie sie heißt, ich weiß nicht, wo sie wohnt.
Ich denke aber noch an ihr Gesicht.

Dunkle Augen, lockiges Haar,
Sag mir jemand, wer sie war.

Das zweite Mal war mitten in der Stadt.
Hat sie mich gesehen? Es könnte sein.
Ich habe ihr nichts gesagt, ich hab' es nicht gewagt.
Dann war sie wieder weg und ich allein.

Dunkle Augen, lockiges Haar,
Sag mir jemand, wer sie war.

Das letzte Mal, das war schon lange her.
Es war ein Nachmittag – ich weiß nicht wann.
Sie ging mit einem Jungen, der älter war als sie.
Er hatte eine Lederjacke an.

Dunkle Augen, lockiges Haar,
Sag mir jemand, wer sie war.

Tipp des Tages

Was hältst du von	Asla?
Wie findest du	Peter?

Ich finde	sie	nett.
		prima.
		toll.
		lieb.
		O.K.
		sympathisch.
	ihn	doof.
		blöd.
		fies.
Ich kann		nicht leiden.
Ich mag		nicht.

sb Selbstbedienung

Lernziel 1

🏴 **So ein Durcheinander!**

Sieh dir die vier Fotos an und lies dann die Formulare.
Welches Foto passt zu welchem Formular?
Beispiel
Jutta – 2

REALSCHULE WALDRUH

Name: Bärbel Müller
Klasse: 9a
Alter: 16
Aussehen: 1,94m groß; ziemlich lange, braune Haare
Adresse: Marktstr. 10, 22926 Ahrensburg
Familienmitglieder: Bruder (3), Schwester (7), Mutter, Vater
Hobbys: Sport, Musik (alles), Briefmarken sammeln, Diskos

REALSCHULE WALDRUH

Name: Bettina Stiegeler
Klasse: 9b
Alter: 15
Aussehen: 1,62m groß; kurze, schwarze Haare
Adresse: Auf der Werde 29, 22927 Großhansdorf
Familienmitglieder: Mutter, Vater, keine Geschwister
Hobbys: Musik (Gitarre), Lesen, Tischtennis, Reisen (Frankreich, Spanien, England), Rad fahren

Beschreib jetzt die vier Mädchen.
Beispiel
Jutta ist mittelgroß und hat lange, schwarze Haare.

REALSCHULE WALDRUH

Name: Jutta Hensel
Klasse: 8b
Alter: 14
Aussehen: 1,60 m groß; lange, schwarz Haare
Adresse: Hermann-Hanke-Str. 45, 22926 Ahrensburg
Familienmitglieder: Mutter, Vater, Bruder (13)
Hobbys: Fotografieren, Reiten, Diskos, mit dem Hund spazieren gehen, Tanzen

REALSCHULE WALDRUH

Name: Anne Meyer
Klasse: 8a
Alter: 14
Aussehen: 1,56 m groß; kurze, blonde Haare
Adresse: Arndorfer Weg 2, 22926 Ahrensburg
Familienmitglieder: Bruder (2), Mutter, Stiefvater
Hobbys: Tennis, Schwimmen, Einkaufen, Ski laufen, Ausgehen

Lernziel 1

 Im Umkleideraum

Sieh dir die Kleider an und lies die Sätze.
Beschrifte die Kleidungsstücke.
Beispiel
A *Karins Hose*

Steffis Hose ist grün.
Karins Hose ist blau.
Sabines Socken sind weiß
Monis Socken sind schwarz.
Juttas Pullover ist rot.
Marias Pullover ist gelb.

Lernziel 2
 Popstar

*Finde ein Bild und beschreib deinen Lieblingssänger/deine Lieblingssängerin.
Wie sieht er/sie aus?
Was trägt er/sie?
Wie findest du ihn/sie?*

Beispiel
Meine Lieblingssängerin heißt Soya Schick. Sie hat lange, schwarze Haare ...

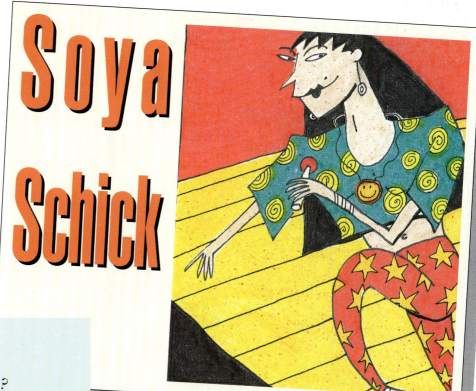

Soya Schick

Lernziel 2
 Quatsch!

*Lies die Sätze. Stimmt das?
Schreib ,das stimmt' oder ,das stimmt nicht'.*
Beispiel
1 *Das stimmt nicht.*

1 Meine beste Freundin
heißt Jutta. Ich finde sie blöd.
2 Mein Deutschlehrer ist unheimlich
nett. Ich finde ihn zu streng.
3 Ich kann meine Sportlehrerin
nicht leiden. Sie ist doof.

4 Mein Bruder hilft nie zu Hause.
Er ist sehr fleißig.
5 Meine Oma ist toll. Ich bekomme
immer jede Menge Taschengeld und
Geschenke von ihr.

Lernziel 2
 Unheimlich bunt!

Kannst du hier fünf Adjektive finden?

I	C	H	B	I	N	T	E	M
D	A	S	Ö	L	F	O	T	O
F	Y	S	H	E	D	S	P	T

Mach weitere bunte Kästen.

Bildvokabeln Im Freibad

ein Pullover

Sandalen

eine Strumpfhose

ein Höschen

ein Minirock

ein BH

ein Badetuch

ein Polohemd

eine Unterhose

eine Badehose

Schuhe

eine Bademütze

Jeans

ein Bikini

Socken

auf einen Blick

1 Asking questions

Wie sieht	er / sie / Anja	aus?	What does	he / she / Anja	look like?

Was hältst du von	Asla? / Peter?	What do you think of	Asla? / Peter?
Wie findest du		What's your opinion of	

2 Describing yourself and others

Ich bin			groß.	I am			tall.
	sehr		klein.		very		small.
Er / Sie	ist	ziemlich	schlank.	He / She	is	quite	slim.
			dick.				fat.
		mittelgroß.				of average height.	

Ich habe	kurze / lange / lockige / glatte	schwarze / braune / blonde / rote	Haare.	I have	short / long / curly / straight	black / brown / blond / ginger	hair.
Er / Sie	hat	kleine / große	braune / blaue / grüne / graue	Augen.	He / She	has	small / large	brown / blue / green / grey	eyes.

3 Talking about what other people are wearing

Anjas / Hasans	Rock / Hemd		blau. / rot. / grün. / weiß. / schwarz.	Anja's / Hasan's	skirt / shirt / pullover / t-shirt / jacket	is	blue. / red. / green. / white. / black.
Sein/Ihr	Pullover / T-Shirt	ist		His/Her			
Seine/Ihre	Jacke			His/Her			
	Schuhe	sind	grau.		shoes	are	grey.

Er / Sie	trägt	einen blauen Pullover. / eine rote Jacke. / ein grünes T-Shirt. / graue Schuhe.	He / She	is wearing	a blue pullover. / a red jacket. / a green t-shirt. / grey shoes.
		eine Brille.			glasses.

4 Expressing opinions about others

Ich finde	sie / ihn	nett. / prima. / toll. / lieb. / O.K. / sympathisch / doof. / blöd. / fies.	I think	she's / he's	nice. / great. / super. / lovely. / OK. / likeable. / stupid. / silly. / horrible.
Ich kann		nicht leiden.	I can't stand him/her.		
Ich mag		nicht.	I don't like him/her.		

Lernziel 1

Kommst du mit?

Partnerarbeit. Hast du Lust?

Lies die Dialoge und erfinde dann Dialoge mit einem Partner/einer Partnerin.

Tag, Werner! Wir gehen gerade zur Eisdiele. Hast du Lust?

Ja, gerne. Ich komme mit.

Tag, Claudia. Was machst du?

Nichts Besonderes.

Hast du Lust, Tischtennis zu spielen?

Ja gut.

Also, komm!

Na, was machen wir?

Hast du Lust, schwimmen zu gehen?

Nee, zu kalt. Ich bleibe lieber hier und spiele Karten.

Hör mal. Wir gehen heute in die Stadt. Kommst du mit?

Nee, ich habe keine Lust.

Kommst du?

Hör gut zu und sieh dir die Bilder an. Was passt wozu?

Beispiel

1 *B*

Wir gehen heute schwimmen. Kommst du mit?

Ja, gerne.

Tipp des Tages

Heute Heute Abend	gebe ich geben wir	eine Party.
Morgen Am Samstag	gehe ich gehen wir	schwimmen. ins Kino. Rollschuh laufen in die Disko.

Kommst du mit?		

Hast du Lust,	mitzukommen? in die Stadt zu fahren? Tennis zu spielen?	

Ja,	gerne. gut.	Ich komme mit.

Nein danke. Ich habe keine Lust.		

Wer kommt mit zur Party?
Lies die Geschichte.

Tag, Irmgard! Sag mal, was machst du morgen Abend?

Ich weiß nicht. Warum?

Na ja ... ich gehe zu einer Party, und ich –

Also viel Spaß. Tschüss!

He! Ursula! Gerd gibt morgen um acht Uhr eine Party. Kommst du mit?

Nein, ich habe keine Lust.

Iris? Hier ist Jens. Möchtest du morgen Abend mit mir –?

Tut mir Leid. Ich gehe aus.

Aber Rolf –

Tut mir Leid. Ich hab' keine Zeit. Tschüss!

Wer kommt mit zu Gerds Party, morgen um acht?

Nein danke. Wir können Gerd nicht leiden.

Na, Jens? Was ist los?

Ach, der arme Gerd. Niemand will zu seiner Party.

Hallo Inge!

Du bist Inge. Lies die Einladungen und sieh dir deinen Terminkalender an. Gehst du oder gehst du nicht? Welche Antwort passt? Schreib es auf.

Beispiel
1 *Ja, gerne.*

1 Am Samstagabend gebe ich eine Party. Kommst du?

2 Wir gehen am Mittwochabend ins Kino. Kommst du mit?

Montag	22	3.00 Krankenhaus! Aua!
Dienstag	23	3.30 Mit Anke Tennis spielen
Mittwoch	24	7.30 Computerklub
Donnerstag	25	8.00 Babysitten
Freitag	26	8.15 Fernsehen: Hitparade Schulaufgaben
Samstag	27	
Sonntag	28	Oma und Opa kommen

3 Ich gehe am Montag nach der Schule einkaufen. Kommst du mit?

4 Am Montagabend gibt es eine Grillparty bei Wagners. Hast du Lust?

5 Wir gehen am Freitagabend in die Disko im Jugendklub. Kommst du?

6 Ich gehe am Dienstagabend zum Jugendklub. Kommst du mit?

7 Willst du am Donnerstagabend bei mir fernsehen?

Tipp des Tages

Tut mir Leid. Da kann ich nicht. Da bin ich leider nicht frei. Leider nicht.		bin krank.	
	Ich	bin krank.	
		habe	keine Lust. keine Zeit.
		muss	zu Hause bleiben. für die Schule arbeiten.
		will	fernsehen. früh ins Bett gehen.

- Tut mir Leid. Da kann ich nicht – ich gehe schon aus.
- Ja, ich komme mit.
- Ja, gerne.
- Da bin ich leider nicht frei – ich muss ins Krankenhaus gehen.
- Ja, ich habe Lust.
- Nein, ich muss zu Hause bleiben.
- Leider nicht, ich will fernsehen.

Die Clique am Samstagabend

Hör gut zu. Was machen die Jugendlichen am Samstagabend?

Beispiel
1 c

Hallo, Christina!

Hallo, Uwe!

Inge?

He, Trudi!

Thomas Schön.

Hallo, Doris!

Frauke Meyer.

Hier ist Jörg.

1 **Uwe ...**
a geht mit Heike aus.
b hat Besuch von seinem Onkel.
c geht zu seiner Schwester.

5 **Inge ...**
a geht in die Stadt.
b arbeitet.
c geht einkaufen.

2 **Christina ...**
a geht zum Jugendklub.
b sieht fern.
c macht ihre Hausaufgaben.

6 **Frauke ...**
a macht ihre Hausaufgaben.
b geht zum Jugendklub.
c geht zu ihrem Freund.

3 **Renate ...**
a bleibt zu Hause.
b geht zum Konzert.
c geht ins Kino.

7 **Stefan ...**
a geht zu Jörg nach Hause.
b geht mit Freunden aus.
c bleibt zu Hause.

4 **Doris ...**
a geht zu Werners Party.
b geht mit Werner aus.
c geht ins Bett.

8 **Trudi ...**
a geht zu Ilses Party.
b geht tanzen.
c geht zu Gabis Party.

Lernziel 2

Wo treffen wir uns?

A

Einladung zu einer Party bei Asaf
Samstag, 10. Nov. gegen 7.30
Berliner Str. 60

B

Rumänisches Staatsballett
‚Schwanensee‘
24. November
In der Stadthalle

C

FUßBALLSPIEL
1. Bundesliga
Blau-Weiß 1890 Berlin
–
Eintracht Frankfurt
4. November
Im Olympiastadion Berlin

D

Geburtstagsfeier bei Susi
Postweg 24
am 11. Nov. um 6 Uhr

E

Grillparty bei Meiers
Kleestraße 7
am 10. November
ab 19.00 Uhr

Wir gehen aus

Hör gut zu.
Diese Jugendlichen gehen alle aus.
Aber wer geht wohin?

Beispiel
Dieter C

F

Alte Oper Bremen
‚Die Wunderstimme aus England‘
Andy Watson und
die Gruppe ‚Fair Play‘

WO?   Im Kleinen Saal
WANN? Samstag, den 12. Dezember um 20.00 Uhr

G

Metal Hammer
die Gruppe mit Pfiff!
Oh Mann oh Mann!

Metal Hammer macht deine
Hirnmasse zum Wackelpudding!

Ohne Metal Hammer bist du
● wie Kaffee ohne Milch
● wie ein Goldfisch ohne Fahrrad
● wie ich ohne meine Freundin

EINTRITT DM 15
BEGINN 20.00 UHR
20. JULI
SPORTHALLE PADERBORN

H

STADTHALLE ALTONA
Samstag, 4. Januar
20 Uhr

PINA
und ihr Orchester
auf Europa-Tournee

Hör nochmal zu. Wo treffen sie sich?

Partnerarbeit. Treffen wir uns vor dem Bahnhof?

Mach Dialoge mit deinem Partner/deiner Partnerin.

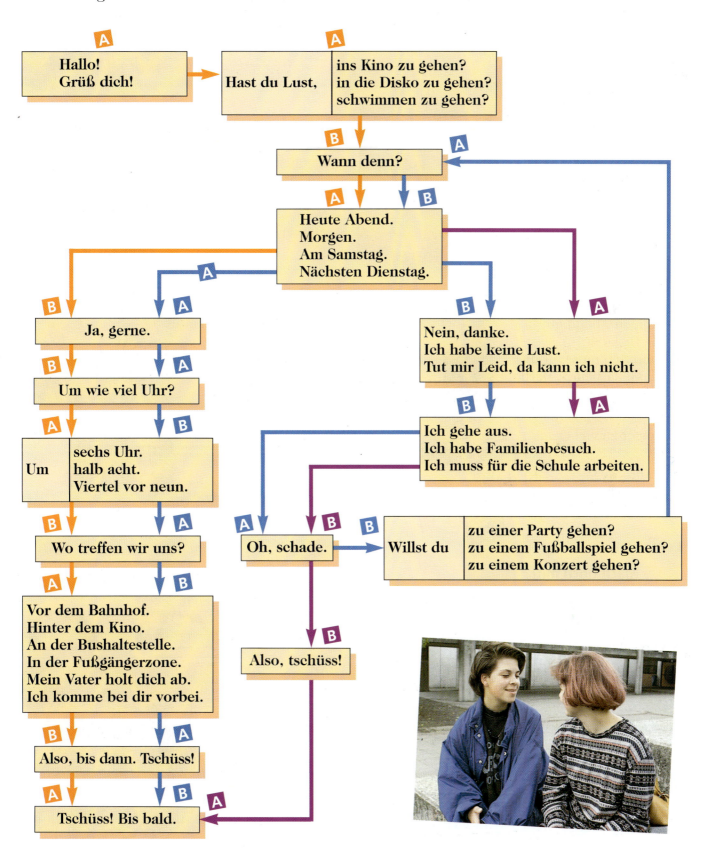

A
Hallo!
Grüß dich!

A
Hast du Lust, | ins Kino zu gehen?
in die Disko zu gehen?
schwimmen zu gehen?

B **A**
Wann denn?

A **B**
Heute Abend.
Morgen.
Am Samstag.
Nächsten Dienstag.

B **A**
Ja, gerne.

B **A**
Nein, danke.
Ich habe keine Lust.
Tut mir Leid, da kann ich nicht.

B **A**
Um wie viel Uhr?

A **B**
Um | sechs Uhr.
halb acht.
Viertel vor neun.

B **A**
Ich gehe aus.
Ich habe Familienbesuch.
Ich muss für die Schule arbeiten.

B **A**
Wo treffen wir uns?

A **B** **B**
Oh, schade.

Willst du | zu einer Party gehen?
zu einem Fußballspiel gehen?
zu einem Konzert gehen?

A **B**
Vor dem Bahnhof.
Hinter dem Kino.
An der Bushaltestelle.
In der Fußgängerzone.
Mein Vater holt dich ab.
Ich komme bei dir vorbei.

B
Also, tschüss!

B **A**
Also, bis dann. Tschüss!

A **B** **A**
Tschüss! Bis bald.

sb *Selbstbedienung*

Lernziel 1

 Schade!

Warum gehen sie nicht mit?
Lies die Dialoge und wähl
die passenden Antworten.

Beispiel
1 *Es kostet zu viel Geld.*

– Du, wir gehen am
  Samstag zum Konzert.
  Kommst du mit?
– Na ja, was kostet das?
– Fünfzig Mark.
– Oh nein, das ist mir zu
  teuer.
– Schade!

2

– Julia, kommst du
  morgen Abend mit in
  die Disko?
– Nein. Ich muss für die
  Klassenarbeit in Mathe
  lernen.

– Heute Nachmittag gehe
  ich schwimmen. Hast
  du Lust mitzukommen?
– Nein, es ist nicht warm
  genug.

4

– Günther und ich
  machen am Donnerstag
  ein Picknick. Kommst
  du mit?
– Nein, ich fahre zu
  meiner Tante.

5

– Jürgen, hast du Lust,
  morgen eine Radtour zu
  machen?
– Nein, mir geht es nicht
  gut.
– Ach schade!

Es kostet zu viel Geld.

Ich fahre weg.

Ich bin krank.

Ich muss für die
Schule arbeiten.

Es ist zu kalt.

Lernziel 1

 Mach doch mit!

Sieh dir die Bilder an und wähl die passenden Antworten aus dem Kasten.

1 Ja, gut.
2 Nein danke. Ich bin allergisch gegen Fisch.
3 Leider nicht. Ich bin Vegetarierin.

Lernziel 1

⚑ Einladungen

Schreib eine Einladung zu einer Party.

Beispiele

Lernziel 2

⚑ Wo treffen sie sich?

Diese Jugendlichen gehen aus.
Lies die Texte und ersetz die Bilder mit den richtigen Wörtern.

Beispiel
1 *Bahnhof*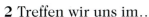

1 Wir treffen uns
   um 8 Uhr vor dem…

2 Treffen wir uns im…

3 Bis heute Abend.
   Acht Uhr vor dem…

4 Radtour um 16 Uhr.
   Treffpunkt vor dem…

5 – Wo treffen wir uns?
   – Vor der…

Lernziel 2

⚑ Telefongespräch

Das Telefongespräch ist total durcheinander.
Schreib es in der richtigen Reihenfolge auf.

– Hallo Dieter! Hier ist Gisela.

– Also, bis dann. Tschüss.

– Gut, danke. Hör mal, am Freitag hat Karin Geburtstag, und sie gibt eine Party. Kommst du?

– Bei mir. Gegen halb acht, O.K.?

– Tschüss.

– Ja, gerne. Vielen Dank. Wo treffen wir uns?

– Na, wie geht's?

– Prima.

🔲 Ausreden

Hör gut zu und lies das Gedicht.

– Kommst du zu meiner Party, Werner?
– Vielen Dank! Ich möchte gerne, aber …

… ich hab' Besuch von meinen Kusinen.
– Umso besser! Komm mit ihnen!

– Ich hab' so viele Hausaufgaben.
– Du hast nicht mehr, als die anderen haben.

– Dann gehe ich mit den Hunden spazieren.
– Kein Problem! Komm' mit den Tieren!

– Ich muss Flöte üben, mit meiner Schwester.
– Toll! Dann bring' das ganze Orchester!

– Ich muss auch babysitten morgen.
– Bring das Kind mit! Keine Sorgen!
– Und noch etwas …

– Was könnte es sein?
– Vielleicht ein kleines, ehrliches ‚Nein'?

1   Asking questions

| Kommst du mit? | Do you want to come along? |

| Hast du Lust, | mitzukommen?
in die Stadt zu fahren?
Tennis zu spielen? | Do you
fancy | coming along
with me?
going into town?
playing tennis? |

| Willst du | zu einer Party
zu einem Fußballspiel
zu einem Konzert | gehen? | Do you
want to | go to a | party?
football match?
concert? |

| Wo treffen wir uns? | Where shall we meet? |

2   Suggesting things to do

| Heute
Heute Abend | gebe ich
geben wir | | eine Party. | Today
This evening | I am throwing
we are throwing | a party. |

| Morgen
Am Samstag | gehe ich
gehen wir | schwimmen.
ins Kino.
Rollschuh laufen.
in die Disko. | Tomorrow
On Saturday | I'm going
we're going | swimming.
to the cinema.
rollerskating.
to the disco. |

3   Accepting and declining invitations

| Ja, | gerne.
gut. | Ich komme mit. | Yes, | I'd like to.
fine. | I'll come with you. |

| Tut mir Leid.
Da kann ich nicht.
Da bin ich leider nicht frei.
Leider nicht. | I'm sorry.
I can't then.
I'm not free then, unfortunately.
Unfortunately not. |

Ich	bin krank.		I	am ill.	
	habe	keine Lust. keine Zeit.		don't fancy it. don't have time.	
	muss	zu Hause bleiben. für die Schule arbeiten.		have to	stay at home. do school work.
	will	fernsehen. früh ins Bett gehen.		want to	watch television. go to bed early.

4   Suggesting where to meet

| Vor dem Bahnhof.
Hinter dem Kino.
An der Bushaltestelle.
In der Fußgängerzone.
Mein Vater holt dich ab.
Ich komme bei dir vorbei. | In front of the station.
Behind the cinema.
At the bus stop.
In the pedestrian precinct.
My father will pick you up.
I'll call round for you. |

Lernziel 1
Krankheiten und Verletzungen

 Partnerarbeit. Was fehlt dir?

Hör gut zu und sieh dir das Diagramm an. Dann mach Dialoge mit deinem Partner/deiner Partnerin.

A
Wir spielen Tennis.
Wir gehen in die Disko.
Wir gehen schwimmen.
Wir gehen ins Kino.

A
Kommst du mit?
Hast du Lust?
Willst du mitkommen?

B
Nein, ich kann nicht.
Nein, ich will nicht.
Leider nicht.
Nein, ich habe keine Lust.

A
Wieso denn?
Warum (denn) nicht?

B
Ich bin krank.
Mir geht's nicht gut.
Mir ist schlecht.
Ich bin nicht gesund.
Ich bin nicht fit.

A
Was fehlt dir?
Was hast du denn?
Was ist mit dir los?

B
Ich habe einen Schnupfen.
Ich habe Fieber.
Ich habe eine Grippe.
Ich habe eine Erkältung.
Ich habe Kopfschmerzen.
Mein Fuß tut weh.
Mein Arm tut weh.
Mein Bein tut weh.

A
Ach, wie schade.
Gute Besserung!
So ein Pech.

 Ich habe Kopfschmerzen ... Mein Fuß tut weh

Hör gut zu. Was passt wozu?

Beispiel
1 *E*

Partnerarbeit. Wer bin ich?

Wähl eine Person und beantworte alle Fragen mit ‚ja' oder ‚nein'.

Beispiel

A – Ja, fertig. Wer bin ich?
B – Hast du Kopfschmerzen?
A – Nein.
B – Hast du Ohrenschmerzen?
A – Ja.

B – Tut dir die Hand weh?
A – Nein.
B – Hast du Zahnschmerzen?
A – Ja.

B – Und hast du auch Fieber?
A – Ja.
B – Du bist Anton.
A – Ja! Jetzt bist du dran.

Tipp des Tages

Was fehlt dir? Was hast du?							
Tut dir	der Kopf der Arm	weh?	Ich habe	Kopfschmerzen. Zahnschmerzen. Magenschmerzen. Rückenschmerzen. Ohrenschmerzen. Halsschmerzen. Fieber. Heuschnupfen.		Mein	Kopf Arm Fuß
				eine	Grippe. Erkältung.	Meine	Hand
				einen	Schnupfen.		

Mein	Kopf Arm Fuß	tut weh.
Meine	Hand	

Ich bin	müde. fit. gesund.

▭ Ich kann nicht ... Ich bin krank

Hör gut zu, sieh dir die Bilder an und beantworte die Fragen. Finde die Wörter im Kasten.

Beispiel
1 *Frank. Sein Fuß tut weh.*

1 Wer kann nicht Fußball spielen?
 Warum nicht?
2 Wer kann nicht in die Schule gehen?
 Warum nicht?
3 Wer kann nicht im Garten arbeiten?
 Warum nicht?
4 Wer kann keine Karotten essen?
 Warum nicht?

Boris

Britta

Maria

Frank

hat	Zahnschmerzen	Sie	Er	hat	weh	Fuß
Magenschmerzen	tut	Kopfschmerzen		Sie	hat	Sein

Entschuldigungszettel

Lies die Zettel und sieh dir die Bilder an. Was passt wozu?

Beispiel
1 *E*

1
19. Oktober
Sehr geehrter Herr Fichte!
Mein Sohn Peter konnte vom 10. bis 14. Oktober wegen einer Erkältung nicht zur Schule gehen.
Mit freundlichen Grüßen
André Fischer

2
Liebe Frau Lach!
Meine Tochter konnte letzte Woche aufgrund hohen Fiebers nicht zur Schule kommen.
Ihre Trudi Timm

4
Liebe Frau Stegemann,
mein Sohn kommt heute wegen einem gebrochenen Fuß nicht in die Schule.
Mit freundlichen Grüßen
Ihr Martin Löschmann

3
Liebe Frau Meier!
Meine Tochter Anita leidet an schweren Zahnschmerzen.
Sie geht heute zum Zahnarzt.
Ihre Frau Ziegert

5
2. April
An den Klassenlehrer der 7B Schlierbach.
Felix Schweiger ist vom 31.3. bis 5.4. wegen eines Krankenhausaufenthaltes (gebrochenes Bein) entschuldigt.

Prim. Dr. med. Meier
Krankenhaus Linz a.d.D.
4020 LINZ
F. Meier

A

B

C

D

E

Lieber Herr Heinemann!

Jetzt bist du dran. Schreib einen
Entschuldigungszettel an deinen Lehrer!

Beispiel

den 5. Mai

Lieber Herr Heinemann!
Mein Sohn Alex konnte
letzte Woche nicht
in die Schule
kommen – er

 Allergien

Hör gut zu.
Welche Allergien
haben die Leute?

Beispiel
1 *D*

1
– Was willst du trinken? Ein Glas Milch?
– Nein, danke. Ich darf nicht.
– Du darfst nicht? Wieso denn?
– Ich bin allergisch gegen Milch. Ich darf
  auch keinen Fisch, keinen Käse, keine
  Sahne und keine Bananen essen.
– Mensch! Das ist ja schlimm!

Tipp des Tages

Hast du Allergien?		
Ich bin allergisch gegen		Tiere. Muscheln. Aspirin. Käse.
Ich darf	keinen Käse keine Schokolade	essen.

Lernziel 2
Medikamente

Haben Sie etwas gegen ...?

Heuschnupfen	Halsschmerzen
Seekrankheit	Schnittwunden
Magenschmerzen	Brandwunden
Ohrenschmerzen	Mücken

◖◗ Partnerarbeit. Haben Sie etwas gegen Seekrankheit?

Wähl eine Krankheit und bitte um ein Medikament dagegen.
Dein(e) Partner(in) muss das beste Medikament empfehlen.

Beispiel
A – Haben Sie etwas gegen Seekrankheit?
B – Ja, hier. Tabletten.

A — Tabletten gegen Seekrankheit
B — eine Packung Hustenbonbons
C — Pflaster
D — ein Spray gegen Mücken
E — Kapseln gegen Heuschnupfen
F — Tropfen gegen Ohrenschmerzen
G — ein Saft gegen Magenschmerzen
H — eine Salbe gegen Brandwunden

 In der Apotheke

Hör gut zu und sieh dir die Bilder oben an. Welches Bild passt?

Beispiel
1 *H*

Haben Sie etwas gegen Zebrastreifen?

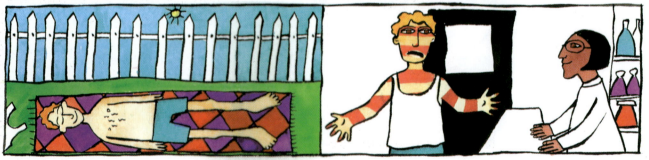

▭ Wundermittel

Sieh dir die Medikamente an und hör gut bei der Werbung zu.
Welches Medikament ist das?
Ist das gegen Ohrenschmerzen oder Kopfschmerzen oder ...?
Schreib es auf.

Beispiel
1 *Heili – gegen Kopfschmerzen*

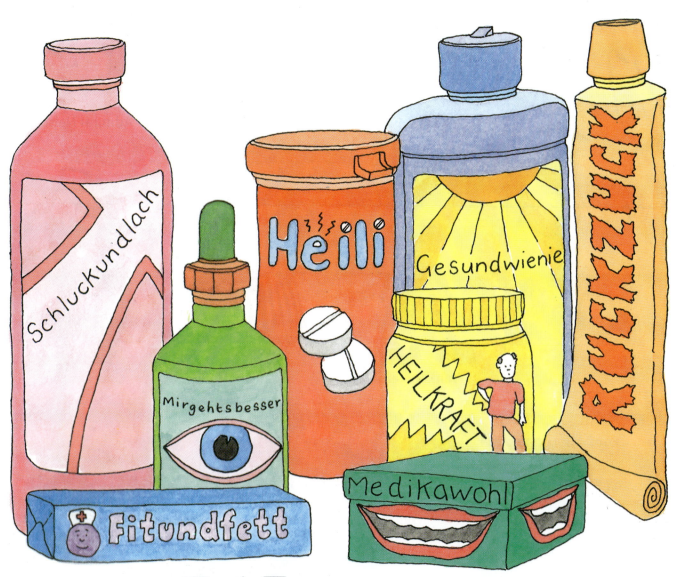

| Haben Sie etwas gegen | Magenschmerzen?
Kopfschmerzen?
Heuschnupfen?
Brandwunden?
Seekrankheit? | Ja, hier. | Tabletten.
Pflaster.
Hustenbonbons.
Kapseln.
Tropfen.
Ein Saft.
Ein Spray.
Eine Salbe. |

sb ▶ Selbstbedienung

Lernziel 1

 Was sagt Long John Silver?

Was sagen diese Leute?
Schreib die Sätze auf.

Beispiel
Long John Silver sagt:
‚Das ist mein Bein.'

Arme   Bein

Ohr   Zähne

Auge   Kopf

Das ist mein ...

Long John Silver

Das sind meine ...

Venus de Milo

Ich sehe keine Schiffe, aber das ist mein ...

Admiral Nelson

Das ist mein ...

Frankenstein

Das ist mein ...

Van Gogh

Das sind meine ...

Graf Dracula

Lernziel 1

 Fünf Minuten später

Sieh dir die Bilder und die Sätze an.
Wer sagt was in fünf Minuten?
Beispiel
A *Ich habe Kopfschmerzen.*

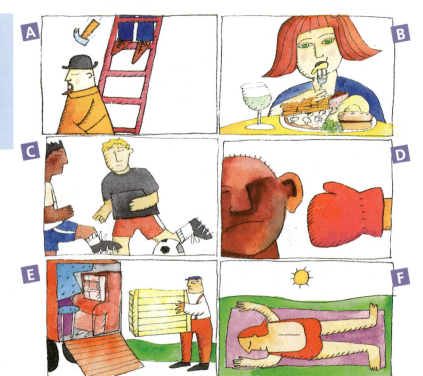

Ich habe Ohrenschmerzen.
Ich habe Kopfschmerzen.
Ich habe einen Sonnenbrand.
Mein Bein tut weh.
Mein Fuß tut weh.
Ich habe Magenschmerzen.

Lernziel 1

 Ich bin allergisch gegen …

*Alle diese Leute haben Allergien.
Was sagen sie?*

Beispiel
*Paul sagt: ‚Ich bin allergisch
gegen Fisch und Tee.'*

Paul

Uschi

Moni

Omri

Sven

Lernziel 2

 Was haben Sie gegen…

*Sieh dir die Werbung
an und lies die Sätze.
Ist das richtig oder
falsch?*

1 Frubienzym ist
gegen
Kopfschmerzen.
2 Carmol ist gegen
Erkältungen.
3 Thomapyrin ist
gegen Fieber.
4 Pulmoll ist gegen
Zahnschmerzen.
5 Rhinopront ist gegen
Schnupfen.

Lernziel 2

 Frank ist krank

*Was fehlt Frank?
Schreib es auf.
Welche Medikamente kannst
du ihm empfehlen?*
Beispiel
*Sein Bein tut weh.
(Schmerztabletten.)*

🎧 Hypochonderlied

Hör zu und sing mit.

Herr Doktor, ich hab' einen Schnupfen.
Sogar meine Augen sind wund.
Können Sie mir etwas geben?
Ich fühle mich gar nicht gesund.

**Nehmen Sie diese Tabletten.
Hoffentlich haben Sie Glück.
Und wenn Sie dann immer noch krank sind,
Kommen Sie in *fünf Tagen* zurück.**

Herr Doktor, ich hab' eine Grippe.
Sogar meine Füße tun weh.
Können Sie mir etwas geben?
Dann nehme ich es mit dem Tee.

**Nehmen Sie diese Tabletten.
Hoffentlich haben Sie Glück.
Und wenn Sie dann immer noch krank sind,
Kommen Sie in *fünf Wochen* zurück.**

Herr Doktor, ich kann gar nicht schlafen.
Seien Sie bitte so nett ...
Ich brauche nur ein paar Tabletten,
Dann gehe ich wieder ins Bett.

**Nehmen Sie diese Tabletten.
Hoffentlich haben Sie Glück.
Und wenn Sie dann immer noch krank sind,
Kommen Sie in *fünf Jahren* zurück!**

Steffi

1 Asking questions

Was fehlt dir? Was hast du? Was ist mit dir los?			What's wrong with you? What have you got? What's your problem?		
Tut dir der	Kopf Arm	weh?	Does your	head arm	hurt?
Hast du Allergien?			*Do you have any allergies?*		
Haben Sie etwas gegen	Magenschmerzen? Kopfschmerzen? Heuschnupfen? Brandwunden? Seekrankheit?		*Do you have anything for*	*stomach ache? headaches? hay fever? burns? sea sickness?*	

2 Talking about illnesses

Ich habe	Kopfschmerzen. Zahnschmerzen. Magenschmerzen. Rückenschmerzen. Ohrenschmerzen. Halsschmerzen. Fieber. Heuschnupfen.		*I've got*	*a headache. toothache. stomach ache. backache. earache. a sore throat. a temperature. hay fever. the flu. a cold. a runny nose.*
	eine	Grippe. Erkältung.		
	einen	Schnupfen.		

Mein	Kopf Arm Fuß	tut weh.	*My*	head arm foot hand	hurts.
Meine	Hand				

Ich bin	müde. fit. gesund.	*I'm*	*tired. fit. healthy.*

3 How to say you've got an allergy

Ich bin allergisch gegen	Tiere. Muscheln. Aspirin. Käse.	*I'm allergic to*	*animals. mussels. aspirin. cheese.*
Ich darf	keinen Käse keine Schokolade	essen.	*I'm not allowed to eat*	*cheese. chocolate.*

4 Understanding what different medicaments are

Ja, hier.	Tabletten. Pflaster. Hustenbonbons. Kapseln. Tropfen. Ein Saft. Ein Spray. Eine Salbe.	*Yes, here you are.*	*Tablets. Plasters. Cough sweets. Capsules. Drops. Medicine. A spray. An ointment.*

Lernziel 1
Wohin?

 Wohin fahren sie?

Diese jungen Leute vom Jugendzentrum Pinneberg planen eine Urlaubsreise. Aber wohin? Und wie kommen sie dahin? Hör zu und lies den Text.

1 Also, bald sind Ferien. Fünf Tage zusammen im Urlaub. Aber wo?

2 Ja, genau. Wohin fahren wir?

3 Nach Spanien – Sonne, Schwimmen und schöne spanische Mädchen!

Lieber schöne spanische Jungen!

4 Oder wie wäre es mit Italien?

Aber nein! Spanien, Italien ... das ist doch alles zu teuer und zu weit! Wir haben nur fünf Tage Urlaub zusammen. Am besten fahren wir gar nicht so weit weg.

5 Ja? Wohin denn?

Nach Helgoland, zum Beispiel!

6 Helgoland? Was gibt's dort Besonderes?

Sonne, Meer, Surfen, viele Touristen ... und keine Autos!

Gruppenarbeit. Und du?

Mach Urlaubspläne.
Wohin fährst du? Und wie fährst du dahin?

Beispiel

A – Ich will nach Schottland fahren.
B – Nein, lieber nicht.
A – Warum nicht?
B – Das ist zu kalt. Fahren wir nach Frankreich.
C – Ja, gut. Wie kommen wir dahin?

D – Mit dem Auto und mit der Fähre?
A – Nein, am besten fliegen wir.
C – Das ist zu teuer.
B – O.K. Fahren wir mit dem Auto und mit der Fähre.

Das stimmt. Helgoland ist autofrei. Und das ist gar nicht so weit von Pinneberg.

Wo liegt das eigentlich?

7

Helgoland ist eine kleine Insel in der Nordsee ... etwa 70 Kilometer von Cuxhaven entfernt.

8

Gute Idee, Volker. Wie kommen wir dorthin? Mit dem Flugzeug?

Lieber nicht. Ich habe immer Flugangst.

Ich fliege ganz gern. Das geht am schnellsten.

Das stimmt, aber es kostet auch am meisten. Mit dem Schiff ist es billiger.

9

10

Oh nein – ich werde immer seekrank!

Du, das ist keine lange Schiffsreise, und das Meer ist ganz ruhig. Wir fahren am besten mit dem Bus nach Cuxhaven und dann direkt mit dem Schiff nach Helgoland.

Na, was meint ihr? Mit dem Bus und dann mit dem Schiff nach Helgoland?

11

12

Ja, klar! Na, gut! O.K.! Toll!

Tipp des Tages

Wohin fahren wir in den Urlaub?		Wie kommen wir am besten dorthin?		
Nach	Spanien. Italien. Helgoland.	Fahren wir mit	dem	Schiff. Bus. Zug. Auto.
			der	Fähre.
Lieber nicht. Das ist zu	weit. kalt. teuer. langweilig.	Am besten fliegen wir.		

Ich	fliege fahre	lieber	mit dem Schiff.	Ich	werde immer seekrank! habe Flugangst!

Mit dem Flugzeug nach Helgoland

*Hör zu und sieh dir die Informationen über
Flüge nach Helgoland an.
Beantworte dann die Fragen.*

HADAG AIR
SOMMERFLUGPLAN

Hamburg – Helgoland – Hamburg

Vorsaison
1. April bis 30. Juni

Hauptsaison
1. Juli bis 31. August

Nachsaison
1. September bis 30. September

HADAG

'ne Brise Urlaub

VORSAISON
1. April bis 30. Juni

HAMBURG – HELGOLAND

verkehrt am	Abflug/Ankunft	Via	Flug
1 2 3 4 5 6	08.15/08.55		
1 2 3 4 5 6 7	17.00/17.40	non-stop	GP 011
1 2 3 4 5 6 7	17.00/18.20	non-stop	GP 015
		GWT	GP 315

HELGOLAND-HAMBURG

verkehrt am	Abflug/Ankunft	Via	Flug
1 2 3 4 5 6	09.10/09.50		
1 2 3 4 5 6 7	18.00/18.40	non-stop	GP 012
1.4.–15.6.		non-stop	GP 016
1 2 3 4 5 6 7 16.6.–30.6.	18.35/19.15	non-stop	GP 316

Zeichenerklärung:
1 – Montag
2 – Dienstag
3 – Mittwoch
4 – Donnerstag
5 – Freitag
6 – Samstag
7 – Sonntag

GP – HADAG AIR Seebäderflug
HGL – Helgoland
GWT – Westerland
HAM – Hamburg

Tagestarif: Hin- und Rückflug an einem Tag

Flugpreise:
HAMBURG-HELGOLAND-HAM – DM 200,- = DM 400,-   Tagestarif: DM 350,-

HADAG AIR   Wir fliegen jeden Tag
Hamburg-Helgoland-Hamburg
Während der Saison mehrmals täglich

Fordern Sie den neuesten Flugplan an

Auskünfte und Buchungen bei Ihrem Reisebüro,
der Kurverwaltung Helgoland oder bei der
HADAG AIR, 22453 Hamburg, Flughafen Tel. (0 40) 50 10 04 / 5
Telex: 02-174496

Buchungen auf Helgoland
Kurverwaltung:	(0 47 25)	7 02 70, Telex: 0232194
Flugplatz:	(0 47 25)	677
Reisebüro Mailänder	(0 47 25)	566

1 Wann beginnt die Vorsaison?
2 Ist der fünfte Juli in der Hauptsaison?
3 Wann ist der erste Flug von Hamburg nach Helgoland?
4 Was kostet eine Rückflugkarte nach Helgoland?
5 Wie lange dauert der Flug?
6 Wie ist die Telefonnummer vom Reisebüro Mailänder?

Mir geht's nicht gut!

📼 Helgoland – Inselparadies!

Volker sitzt bequem und beschreibt Helgoland.
Sieh dir den Text und die Bilder an und hör zu.
Ersetz die Bilder mit den passenden Wörtern
aus dem Kasten unten.

1

Helgoland ist eine kleine in der Nordsee. Sie besteht aus

drei Teilen: Oberland, Unterland und Düne. In Oberland sieht man die

schönen roten am Meer.

2

Im Südosten liegt Unterland, und im Osten befindet sich die zweite,

kleinere Insel von Helgoland: Düne. Hier ist der ⬭ schön weiß,

und viele Leute schwimmen, 🏄, segeln und 🪂. Es gibt

sogar einen 🏖️FKK, wo sich die Leute nackt sonnen und schwimmen!

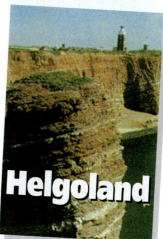

Helgoland

3

Aber auch wenn die ☀️ scheint, ist es oft windig am Strand, und

viele Leute sitzen im 🧺 oder in den ⛰️ und sonnen sich.

4

Auf Helgoland kann man 🏌️ und 🎾 spielen.

Abends kann man auch in die 🕺 gehen.

5

Außerdem ist Helgoland ⚠️ und 🧺ZOLL. Viele Touristen

besuchen Helgoland nur für einen Tag und machen Einkäufe, denn Tabak,

, , Tee, , und Fleisch

sind dort billiger als in Deutschland.

Strandkorb	**Insel**	**Käse**	**Disko**	**Minigolf**
Sonne	**Felsen**	**Dünen**	**Strand** **autofrei**	
Tennis	**angeln**	**Kaffee**		
Wein	**surfen**	**Parfüm**	**zollfrei**	**Sand**

Lernziel 2
Camping macht Spaß!

 Welcher Campingplatz?

Hör zu, lies die Texte und sieh dir diese Campingplätze an.
Welcher Campingplatz ist für welche Gruppe am besten geeignet?

Beispiel
1 *Familie Leiser – Campingplatz Schöndorf*

CAMPINGPLATZ SCHÖNDORF
80 Stellplätze
Einrichtungen:
Wasch- u. Toilettenräume • Kinderspielplatz
• beheiztes Schwimmbad • Minigolf
In der Nähe:
Wassersport • Angeln • Reiten
• Tennis • Trimm-dich-Pfad
Hunde nicht gestattet

Campingplatz Zauberberg
75 ruhige Stellplätze
Einrichtungen:
Warme Duschen   WC
Supermarkt   Tennisplatz
Spielfeld für Volleyball u.
Federball   Schwimmbad
Tischtennis
In der Nähe:
Wanderungsmöglichkeiten
Rundfahrten in den Bergen

CAMPINGPLATZ RUHEWALD
60 Stellplätze
Einrichtungen:
Waschräume ▪ WC ▪ warme Duschen ▪ Restaurant
▪ Supermarkt ▪ Kinderspielplatz ▪ Bootsverleih
▪ Schwimmbad u. Kinderschwimmbecken
In der Nähe:
Wanderwege   Hunde gestattet

CAMPINGPLATZ KLEINER BLAUSEE
30 Stellplätze
Einrichtungen:
Warme Duschen   WC   Supermarkt   Badesee   Angeln
Wassersport   Kegeln   Minigolf
In der Nähe:
Surfen   eigener Strand

Campingplatz Rosenstadt
65 Stellplätze
Einrichtungen:
Duschen ● WC
● Supermarkt ● beheiztes
Schwimmbad ● eigener
Strand ● Bar mit Disko
● Jugendraum

CAMPINGPLATZ DONAUINSEL
120 Stellplätze
Einrichtungen:
Waschgelegenheit   Duschen
WC   Restaurant   Schnellimbiss
Bar   Schwimmbad   2 Tennisplätze
Kinderspielplatz
In der Nähe:
Touristik   Rundfahrten
Sehenswürdigkeiten

---

1 **Die Familie Leiser**

Wir sind alle sehr sportlich. Ich will Tennis spielen. Mein Sohn Markus will angeln und mein Mann auch. Meine Töchter wollen reiten, und ich will jeden Tag schwimmen.

2 **Drei Teenager: Tulai, Asla und Jutta**

Ich will andere junge Leute treffen. Meine Freundinnen Asla und Jutta auch. Das ist sehr wichtig für uns. Wir schwimmen auch alle sehr gern.

3 **Zwei Studenten aus der Schweiz: Peter und Jens**

Ich will die Gegend besuchen und Ausflüge machen. Wir wollen aber auf dem Campingplatz essen – wir kochen nicht so gern!

4 **Die Familie Strotmann**

Meine Tochter und mein Sohn schwimmen sehr gern und wollen auch Wassersport treiben. Wir wollen lieber einen Campingplatz an der See. Mein Mann und ich sind keine Diskofans. Am liebsten wollen wir einen kleineren, ruhigen Campingplatz.

5 **Die Familie Blumenauer**

Wir wollen einen schönen Campingplatz finden, wo unser vierjähriger Sohn Philip ruhig spielen kann. Wir bringen auch unseren Hund Max mit. Ich will ein paar Wanderungen machen.

6 **Zwei Teenager: Meike und Ralf**

Ich will unbedingt viel Sport treiben, und meine Freundin Meike will viele Wanderungen machen. Wir sind nämlich sehr sportlich. Wir hassen aber Diskos!

Und du?

Wähl einen Campingplatz und sag, warum er für dich am besten geeignet ist.

Beispiel
Campingplatz Rosenstadt – es gibt einen Jugendraum, eine Disko und ein Schwimmbad.

🔵🔵 Partnerarbeit. Auf dem Campingplatz

Du kommst am Campingplatz Nürnberg an.
Lies den Text, dann mach Dialoge und ersetz
die Wörter in Blau durch andere Wörter.

Beispiel

A – Guten Tag. Haben Sie noch Plätze frei?
B – Ja. Wie lange wollen Sie bleiben?
A – Eine Nacht.
B – Und wie viele Personen sind Sie?
A – Zwei Erwachsene und zwei Kinder.
B – Wie alt sind die Kinder?
A – Acht und dreizehn.
B – Haben Sie einen Wohnwagen?
A – Nein, wir haben ein Auto und ein Zelt.
B – Also, zwei Erwachsene und zwei Kinder mit
    Auto und Zelt für eine Nacht – das macht 35
    Mark 50.

Bist du ein Genie in Mathe?

Kannst du gut rechnen?
Sieh dir die Preisliste nochmal an.
Was kostet es für diese Familien auf dem
Campingplatz Nürnberg?

1	für 2 Nächte
2	für 1 Nacht
3	für 3 Nächte
4	für 4 Nächte
5	für 2 Nächte

Beispiel 1

Ein Zelt und PKW = DM 10,50 × 2 = DM 21,00
Zwei Erwachsene = DM 16,00 × 2 = DM 32,00
Ein Kind   = DM 4,50 × 2 = DM 9,00
Gesamtsumme   = DM 62,00

Campingplatz Nürnberg
Volkspark Dutzendteich

PREISLISTE

Preis je Person und Nacht

Erwachsene	DM 8,00
Kinder (3-14 Jahre)	DM 4,50
Wohnwagen mit PKW	DM 10,50
Campingbus	DM 10,50
Zelt und PKW	DM 10,50
Zelt	DM 8,00

Der große Campingplatz verfügt über 200
Einheiten zu je 100 qm. Während der
Hauptreisezeit steht den Gästen eine
Cafeteria zur Verfügung. Außerdem gibt es
auf dem Campingplatz genügend
Warmwasserduschen, eine Waschmaschine,
einen Wäschetrockner und einen
Autowaschplatz.

Tipp des Tages

Haben Sie noch Plätze frei?		
Ich will Wir wollen	eine Nacht zwei Nächte eine Woche	bleiben.

Wir sind	zwei drei vier	Erwachsene	und	ein zwei drei	Kind. Kinder.

Ich habe Wir haben	ein	Auto. Zelt.
	einen	Wohnwagen. Campingbus.
	eine	Reservierung.

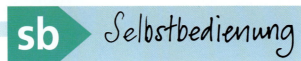 **sb** ▶ *Selbstbedienung*

Lernziel 1

 Mein idealer Urlaub

Wohin willst du am liebsten fahren? Zeichne ein Poster von deinem idealen Urlaubsziel.

Beispiel

Lernziel 1

 Bus-Schiffsreise nach London

Lies den Text, füll die Lücken aus und schreib die Sätze in der richtigen Reihenfolge auf.

Lernziel 1

 Lieber nicht!

Lies die Bildgeschichten und füll die leere Sprechblase aus.

Jetzt schreib (und zeichne!) ähnliche Bildgeschichten.

26.-28.10.

Bus-Schiffsreise nach London
inkl. 1 Übernachtung/Frühstück nur DM 400,-

Die Themse-Metropole London ist Ziel einer 2 ½-tägigen Bus-Schiffsreise vom Freitag, den 26.10 bis zum Sonntag, den 28.10. Für nur 400 Mark pro Person können Sie, verehrte Blitz-Tipp-Leser dabei sein!

Hier der Reiseverlauf in Kürze:

Freitag, 26.10. 20 Uhr Abfahrt in Frankfurt/Main, 21.45 Uhr Abfahrt in Mainz und um 22 Uhr Abfahrt in Wiesbaden. Fahrt über die Autobahn Köln-Aachen nach Calais.

Samstag, 27.10. Am frühen Morgen Ankunft in Calais und anschließend Überfahrt nach Dover. Danach Weiterfahrt in die britische Hauptstadt.

Ankunft gegen Mittag. Der Rest des Tages steht Ihnen zur freien Verfügung. Übernachtung im Hotel.

Sonntag, 28.10.. Nach dem Frühstück Rückfahrt über Dover-Calais in das Rhein-Main-Gebiet, das wir am späten Sonntagabend wieder erreichen werden.

A Am frühen Morgen am 27. Oktober erreicht man ...

B Am 28. Oktober fährt man nach dem Frühstück wieder nach ... und kommt spät am Abend an.

C Dann überquert man den Britischen Kanal nach ... und kommt gegen ... in London an.

D Am 26. Oktober um neun Uhr abends fährt man mit dem ... von Frankfurt am Main ab.

Lernziel 2

 Campingplatzregeln

Sieh dir die Bilder und Regeln an.
Wie sind die Regeln richtig?
Und welches Bild passt zu welcher Regel?

Beispiel
A *Keine laute Musik*

> Nicht schneller
> Keine laute
> für ihre Kinder
> Ruhe
> Eltern haften
> Ab 22 Uhr absolute
> Musik
> als 10 km fahren

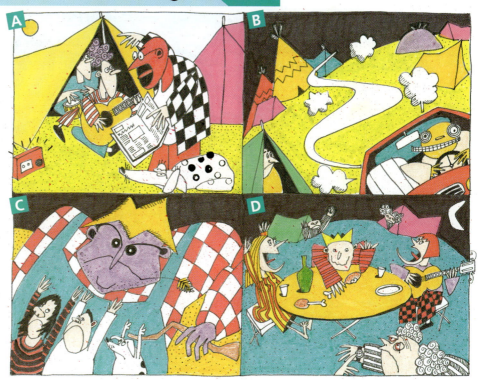

Lernziel 2

 Camping – ja oder nein?

Was hältst du von Camping? Schreib deine Meinung auf und begründe sie.

Beispiele

Camping ist toll – es ist gesund und billig und macht Spaß.

Camping? Lieber nicht! Das ist so langweilig. Ich hasse Campingplätze!

Lernziel 2

 Wir haben eine Reservierung

Welche Antwort passt zu welcher Frage?

Beispiel
1 *e*

1 Haben Sie noch Plätze frei?
2 Wie lange wollen Sie bleiben?
3 Wie viele Personen sind sie?
4 Wie alt sind die Kinder?
5 Haben sie einen Wohnwagen?
6 Haben sie ein Zelt?
7 Kann ich Ihnen helfen?
8 Ist Ihr Sohn unter fünfzehn?

a Zwei Erwachsene und zwei Kinder.
b Nein, einen Wohnwagen.
c Ja, der ist vierzehn.
d Ja.
e Ja, es ist im Moment noch viel frei.
f Ja, wir haben eine Reservierung für heute Nacht.
g Eine Nacht.
h Elf und dreizehn.

Bildvokabeln

Auf dem Campingplatz

der Bootsverleih

Stellplätze für Zelte

die Kegelbahn

die Grillhütte

der Schnellimbiss

Waschräume

das Geschäft

Waschmaschinen und Wäschetrockner

der Kinderspielplatz

das Büro/die Anmeldung

🔊 Urlaubszeit

Hör zu und lies das Gedicht.

Die Welt ist weit,
Urlaubszeit.
Keine Arbeit,
Glückseligkeit.

Sonnenlicht
Im Gesicht.
Denke nicht,
Kein Unterricht.

Wenig Geld,
Altes Zelt,
Freies Feld,
Weite Welt.

1 Asking questions

Wohin fahren wir?	Where shall we go?
Wie kommen wir am besten dorthin?	What's the best way to get there?
Haben Sie noch Plätze frei?	Have you got any spaces free?

auf einen Blick

2 Saying what you'd rather do and why

Fahren wir nach	Spanien. Helgoland.	Let's go to	Spain. Helgoland.

Lieber nicht! Das ist zu	weit. teuer. kalt. warm.	I'd rather not! It's too	far. expensive. cold. hot.

Ich	fahre	lieber	mit dem Schiff.	I prefer	to travel by boat.
	fliege	lieber.			to fly.

Am besten fliegen wir.	It's best if we fly.

Ich	habe Flugangst. werde immer seekrank.	I am afraid of flying. I always get seasick.

3 Saying what you want to do on holiday

Ich will Wir wollen	eine Nacht zwei Nächte	bleiben.	I We	want to	stay	for one night. for two nights.
		schwimmen.			swim.	
	junge Leute	treffen.			meet young people.	
		reiten.			go riding.	
	viel Sport	treiben			do lots of sport.	
	Ausflüge	machen.			go out on trips.	
	auf dem Campingplatz	essen.			eat on the campsite.	

4 Booking into a campsite

Wir sind	zwei drei vier	Erwachsene	und	ein	Kind.	We are	two three four	adults	and	one	child.
				zwei drei	Kinder.					two three	children.

Ich habe Wir haben	ein	Auto. Zelt.	I have We have	a	car. tent.
	einen	Wohnwagen. Campingbus.			caravan. camper van.
	eine	Reservierung.			reservation.

Lernziel 1
Im Kaufhaus

🔊 **Wegweiser**

In einem Kaufhaus kann man fast alles kaufen.
Sieh dir den Wegweiser an.
Hör zu. In welchem Stock findet man jeden Artikel?

Beispiel
1 *Im Erdgeschoss*

WEGWEISER

ZWEITER STOCK	**2**
Möbel	
Teppiche	
Bettwäsche	
Spielwaren	

ERSTER STOCK	**1**
Damenmode	
Herrenmode	
Schuhe	
Mode für Jugendliche	
Kindermode	

ERDGESCHOSS	**E**
Andenken	
Schreibwaren	
Sportartikel	
Geschenke	
Schmuck	
Musik: Kassetten und CDs	
Videokassetten	

UNTERGESCHOSS	**U**
Alles für den Garten	
Pflanzen und Blumen	
Lebensmittel	

👄 **Partnerarbeit. Wo kann ich hier ... bekommen?**

Mach Dialoge in einem Kaufhaus.
Partner(in) A arbeitet im Kaufhaus, und Partner(in) B bittet um Hilfe.

Beispiel
B – Entschuldigung. Wo kann ich hier CDs bekommen?
A – Im Erdgeschoss.

Partnerarbeit. Wo ...?

Hier ist ein großes, modernes Kaufhaus.
Partner(in) A denkt an einen Artikel. Aber an welchen?
Partner(in) B stellt Fragen, Partner(in) A antwortet mit ‚ja' oder ‚nein'.

Beispiel

B – Ist dieser Artikel im Erdgeschoss? B – Ist er im zweiten Stock? B – Ein Sofa?
A – Nein. A – Ja. A – Ja! Jetzt bist du dran.

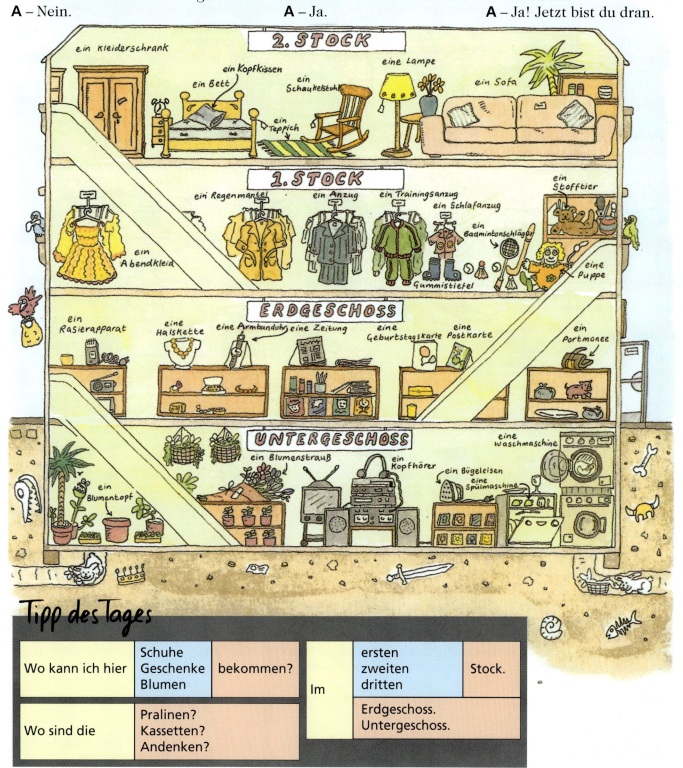

Tipp des Tages

Wo kann ich hier	Schuhe Geschenke Blumen	bekommen?	Im	ersten zweiten dritten	Stock.
Wo sind die	Pralinen? Kassetten? Andenken?			Erdgeschoss. Untergeschoss.	

Preissensationen

Du hast tausend Mark gewonnen!
Was kaufst du im Kaufhaus?
Sieh dir die Artikel an und mach eine Liste.
Du darfst nicht mehr als tausend Mark
ausgeben!

CDs
CM 160,-

eine Gitarre
DM 225,-

ein Radiorekorder
DM 300,-

ein Fernseher
DM 420,-

ein CD-Spieler
DM 200,-

ein Taschenrechner
DM 30,-

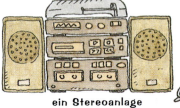

ein Stereoanlage
DM 425,-

Skier
DM 600,-

eine
Videokamera
DM 800,-

ein Fotoapparat
DM 525,-

ein Computer
DM 1000,-

Video-
und
Computerspiele
DM 500,-

ein Fahrrad
DM 500,-

Kleider
DM 400,-

Tipp des Tages

Was kaufst du?			Ist das billig oder teuer?	
Ich kaufe	einen	Taschenrechner.	Das ist	billig. preiswert. teuer. Wucher!
	eine	Gitarre.		
	ein	Fahrrad.		
	Kleider.			

Sportausrüstung
DM 800,-

Lernziel 2
Schenken und Schicken

Partnerarbeit. Geschenke

Du bist mit deinem Partner/deiner Partnerin in einem Kaufhaus. Du willst einige Geschenke kaufen. Mach Dialoge.

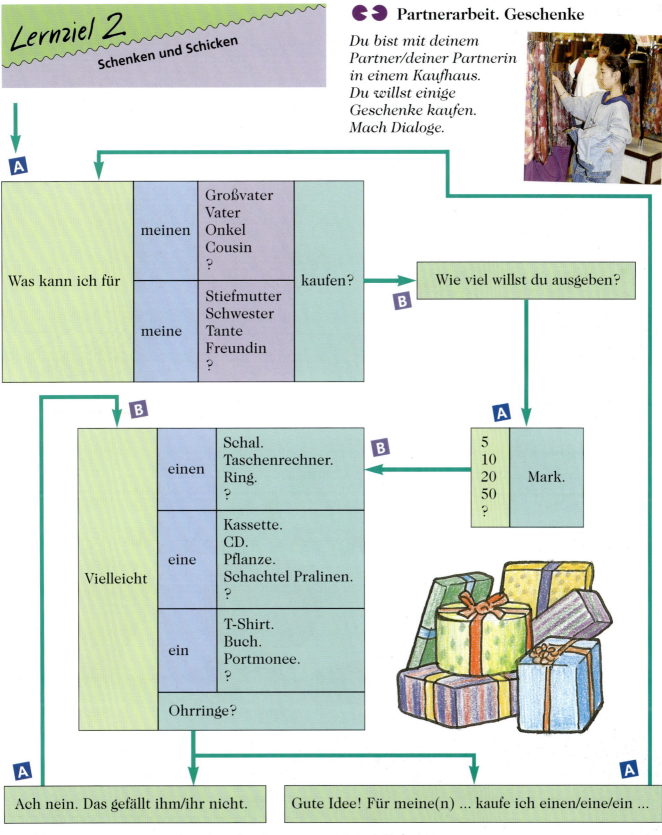

A

Was kann ich für	meinen	Großvater Vater Onkel Cousin ?	kaufen?
	meine	Stiefmutter Schwester Tante Freundin ?	

B → Wie viel willst du ausgeben?

A

	5 10 20 50 ?	Mark.

B

Vielleicht	einen	Schal. Taschenrechner. Ring. ?
	eine	Kassette. CD. Pflanze. Schachtel Pralinen. ?
	ein	T-Shirt. Buch. Portmonee. ?
	Ohrringe?	

A Ach nein. Das gefällt ihm/ihr nicht.

A Gute Idee! Für meine(n) ... kaufe ich einen/eine/ein ...

Mach jetzt eine Liste von den Geschenken.

Beispiel

Für meine Tante kaufe ich einen Schal.

Partnerarbeit. Gefällt es dir?

Sieh dir die Kleider an.
Wie findest du sie?

Beispiel

A – Gefällt dir die Bluse?
B – Ja, das gefällt mir. Gefallen dir die Schuhe?
A – Nein, die Schuhe gefallen mir nicht.

Und die Geschenke?

Wer mag sein/ihr Geschenk?
Wer mag es nicht? Schreib es auf.

Beispiel

A Der Schal gefällt meiner Mutter.

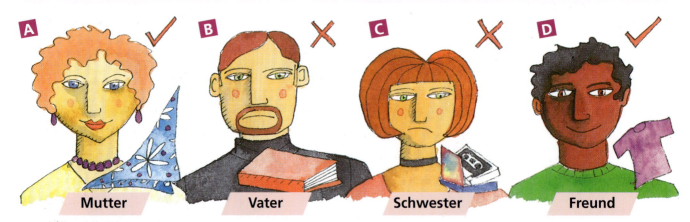

| A Mutter | B Vater | C Schwester | D Freund |

Tipp des Tages

Gefällt es dir?			Das gefällt mir (nicht).		
Gefällt	dir deinem Vater deiner Mutter	der Schal? die Kassette? das Buch?	Der Pullover Die Bluse Das Hemd	gefällt	mir meinem Vater meiner Mutter	(nicht).
Gefallen		die Handschuhe?	Die Schuhe	gefallen		

🔊 Auf der Post

Sieh dir die Briefe und Postkarten an und hör gut zu.
Was passt wozu?

Beispiel
1 *D*

1 – Was kostet eine Postkarte nach Frankreich, bitte?
 – Achtzig Pfennig.
 – Und ein Brief?
 – Eine Mark.
 – Also, eine zu 80 Pfennig und eine zu einer Mark.

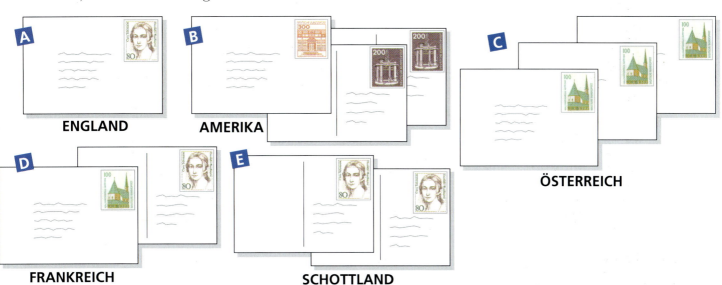

A ENGLAND

B AMERIKA

C ÖSTERREICH

D FRANKREICH

E SCHOTTLAND

Informationen am Briefkasten

Briefkastenleerung				
	15.15	17.00	18.30	19.30
Montag - Freitag	15.15	17.00	18.30	19.30
Samstag	11.45			

Sendungen mit Eilzustellung bitte bei den Postämtern einliefern

Nächster Briefkasten mit weiteren Leerungen			
Standort	Mo - Fr	Sa	So
Wittekindstr. 5-8			9.45
Postamt am Bahnhof	7.00	7.00	12.00
	22.00		

Tipp des Tages

Was kostet	eine Postkarte ein Brief	nach	England? Österreich? Schottland? Amerika?
Eine Briefmarke Zwei Briefmarken	zu	80 Pfennig, einer Mark,	bitte.

Du willst jetzt deine Briefe und Postkarten abschicken.
Du suchst dir einen Briefkasten aus.
Verstehst du die Informationen?
Lies die Sätze und schreib 'richtig' oder 'falsch'.

1 Die Briefkästen in Deutschland sind gelb.
2 Man steckt einen Brief für Hamburg in den rechten Kasten ein.
3 Sonntags gibt es hier die meisten Leerungen.
4 Es ist Samstagabend. Die nächste Leerung ist am Montagmorgen.
5 Am Donnerstag leert man diesen Briefkasten dreimal.

sb ▸ Selbstbedienung

Lernziel 1

🚩 **Was ist das?**

Sieh dir die Geschenke an und wähl die passenden Wörter aus dem Kästchen.

Beispiel
1 *Fußballschuhe*

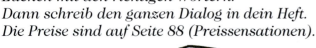

> ein Badmintonschläger
> eine Puppe
> Fußballschuhe
> ein Bleistift
> eine Pflanze
> ein Portmonee

Lernziel 1

🏴 **He Axel, was kostet ...?**

Sieh dir die Bilder und die Lücken im Text an.
Ersetz die Bilder und die Lücken mit den richtigen Wörtern.
Dann schreib den ganzen Dialog in dein Heft.
Die Preise sind auf Seite 88 (Preissensationen).

– He Axel, was kostet ?

– Vier... Mark.

– Das ist aber teuer! Und  ?

– ...hundert Mark. Du,  ist aber preiswert!

– Du hast doch einen CD-Spieler!

– Ja, stimmt. Acht... Mark für  , das ist Wucher!

– Was ... denn ?

– ... Mark.

– Mensch, das ist alles so t...! Und ich mit meinen zwanzig Mark Taschengeld!

Lernziel 1

🚩 **Tierheim**

Wo wohnen die Tiere?
Schreib den richtigen Stock auf.

Beispiel
Das Eichhörnchen wohnt im zweiten Stock.

Lernziel 1

 Kaufhaus BILLIG

Zeichne ein Poster und mach Werbung für:
Kaufhaus PREISWERT, Kaufhaus TEUER oder Kaufhaus WUCHER.

Beispiel

Lernziel 2

 Briefmarken

Schreib folgenden Dialog auf der Post in der richtigen Reihenfolge auf.

– Auf Wiedersehen.
– Ja.
– Eine Mark.
– Guten Tag.
– 80 Pfennig.
– Danke schön. Auf Wiedersehen.
– Eine Briefmarke zu 80 Pfennig und zwei zu einer Mark.
– Nach Wales?
– Guten Tag. Was kostet ein Brief nach Wales?
– Und eine Postkarte?
– Bitte schön – das macht zwei Mark 80.

Lernziel 2

 Was kaufst du für ...?

Sieh dir die Bilder an. Schreib Sätze.

Beispiel
Für meine Mutter kaufe ich eine Pflanze.

Mutter

Bruder

Stiefschwester

Onkel

Großmutter

 Gefällt deiner Mutter ihr Geschenk? Und deinem Vater? Schreib es auf.

Beispiel
Die Pflanze gefällt meiner Mutter.

Kleiner Mensch

Hör zu und sing mit.

Letzte Woche hatte ich Geburtstag.
Man hat mir einen neuen Walkman geschenkt.
Plötzlich sah ich einen kleinen Menschen,
Der sagte mir, was er darüber denkt.

Refrain:

‚Denke
Nicht immer an Geschenke,
Denke
Nicht immer nur an Geld.
Was haben dir
Deine Eltern gegeben?
Das Leben! Ja, das Leben!
Das beste Geschenk auf der Welt!'

Letzte Woche sah ich meinen Onkel.
Er hat mir ein Computerspiel geschenkt.
Plötzlich hörte ich den kleinen Menschen.
Der sagte mir, was er darüber denkt.

Refrain

Letzte Woche war ich bei Verwandten.
Man hat mir hundertneunzig Mark geschenkt.
Plötzlich sah ich da den kleinen Menschen.
Ihr wisst schon, was er darüber denkt.

Refrain

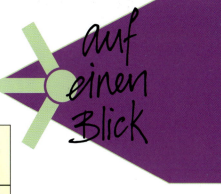

1 Asking questions

Was kaufst du?	*What are you buying?*
Wo kann ich hier Geschenke bekommen?	*Where are the gifts?*
Wo sind die Kassetten?	*Where are the cassettes?*
Wie viel willst du ausgeben?	*How much do you want to spend?*
Gefällt es dir?	*Do you like it?*

Gefällt	dir deinem Vater deiner Mutter	der Schal? die Kassette? das Buch?	*Do you* *Does your father* *Does your mother*	*like*	*the scarf?* *the cassette?* *the book?*
Gefallen		die Handschuhe?			*the gloves?*

Ist das billig oder teuer?	*Is it cheap or expensive?*

Was kostet	eine Postkarte ein Brief	nach	Österreich? Schottland?	*What is the price of*	*a postcard* *a letter*	*to*	*Austria?* *Scotland?*

2 Saying which floor things are on

Im	ersten zweiten dritten	Stock.	*On the*	*first* *second* *third*		*floor.*
	Erdgeschoss.			*ground*		
	Untergeschoss.		*In the*	*basement.*		

3 Saying what you are going to buy and for whom

Für	meinen Vater meine Mutter	kaufe ich	einen Taschenrechner. eine Pflanze.	*I am buying*	*a calculator* *a plant*	*for*	*my father.* *my mother.*

4 Commenting on prices

Das ist	billig. preiswert. teuer Wucher!	*That's*	*cheap.* *good value.* *expensive.* *a rip off!*

5 Saying you like/dislike something

Das gefällt mir (nicht).	*I (don't) like it.*

Der Pullover Die Bluse Das Hemd	gefällt	mir meinem Vater meiner Mutter	(nicht).	*I* *My father* *My mother*	*(don't) like* *likes (doesn't like)*	*the pullover.* *the blouse.* *the shirt.*
Die Schuhe	gefallen					*the shoes.*

6 Buying stamps

Eine Briefmarke Zwei Briefmarken	zu	90 Pfennig, einer Mark zehn,	bitte.	*One stamp* *Two stamps*	*at*	*90 Pfennig,* *one mark ten,*	*please.*

10 Ein tolles Jahr!

Hör gut zu und sieh dir Sabines Fotoalbum an.
Welches Foto passt zu welchem Satz?

Beispiel
Januar – 5

1 Ich bin zu einer neuen Schule gegangen.

3 Ich bin mit meiner Familie in den Schwarzwald gefahren.

2 Ich habe auch einen Job als Babysitter bekommen.

4 Ich habe zum Geburtstag ein neues Fahrrad bekommen.

5 Ich bin nach Australien ins Barossatal zu meiner Großmutter geflogen.

6 Ich habe mir beim Skifahren das Handgelenk gebrochen.

7 Ich habe Omri kennen gelernt.

8 Ich habe auch eine Klassenfahrt nach England gemacht.

9 Ich habe Weihnachten gefeiert.

10 Ich habe viel Tennis gespielt.

11 Ich habe für die Schule viel gearbeitet.

12 Ich habe für Partys neue Klamotten gekauft.

Tipp des Tages

Was hast du	letztes Jahr		gemacht?
	im	Mai Oktober Dezember	

Ich habe	viel Tennis	gespielt.
	eine Klassenfahrt	gemacht.
	mir das Handgelenk	gebrochen.
	ein neues Fahrrad	bekommen.
Ich bin	zu einer neuen Schule	gegangen.
	nach Australien	geflogen.

◖◗ **Partnerarbeit**

Beispiel
A – Du bist Sabine. Ich stelle die Fragen, O.K.?
B – Ja.
A – Was hast du im Mai gemacht?
B – Ich habe viel Tennis gespielt.

Januar

Februar

März

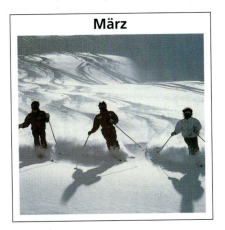

April

Mai

Juni

Juli

August

September

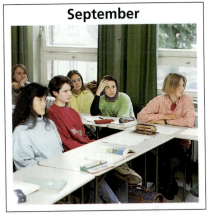

Oktober

November

Dezember

IM FEBRUAR

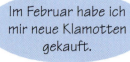 **Was hast du heute gekauft?**

Hör gut zu. Was haben diese Jugendlichen gekauft?

Beispiel
Heike H, E

Im Februar habe ich mir neue Klamotten gekauft.

Heike

Susi

A Ohrringe

B Turnschuhe
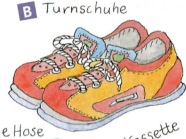

C einen Computer

D eine Hose

E eine Kassette

Peter

Rebekka

F Sachen für die Schule

G einen Pullover

H ein Make-up

 Partnerarbeit. Was hast du gestern gekauft?

Beispiel
A – Heute ist Mittwoch. Was hast du gestern gekauft?
B – Ich habe gestern einen Pullover und ein Buch gekauft.

| Sonntag | Montag | Dienstag | Mittwoch |

| Donnerstag | Freitag | Samstag |

Tipp des Tages

Was hast du	heute gestern	gekauft?	
Ich habe	einen	Computer Pullover	gekauft.
	eine	Hose Kassette	
	ein	Eis Make-up	
	Sachen für die Schule		

IM APRIL

Partnerarbeit. Was hast du zu deinem Geburtstag bekommen?

Sieh dir die Bilder an und mach ein Kettenspiel mit einem Partner/einer Partnerin.

Im April habe ich zum Geburtstag ein neues Fahrrad bekommen.

Beispiel
A – Ich habe eine Gitarre bekommen.
B – Ich habe eine Gitarre und einen Tennisschläger bekommen.
A – Ich habe ...

Was hast du an deinem Geburtstag gemacht?

Sieh dir die Bilder und die Texte an und hör gut zu. Was passt wozu?

Beispiel
Sabine D

Sabine — Ich habe eine Party gegeben.

Ich bin ins Kino gegangen. **Michael**

Tulai — Ich habe Freunde getroffen, und wir haben ein Eis gegessen.

Ich habe Tennis gespielt. **Miriam**

Jutta — Ich bin zu einer Freundin gegangen. Wir haben Kuchen gegessen.

Ich bin zu Hause geblieben, hab' ferngesehen. **Kai**

Tipp des Tages

Was hast du zum Geburtstag bekommen?		
Ich habe	einen Drucker eine Gitarre ein Buch Geld Kleider	bekommen.

Was hast du	an deinem Geburtstag gestern Abend	gemacht?
Ich habe	eine Party	gegeben.
	einen Film	gesehen.
	ein paar Freunde	getroffen.
	Tennis	gespielt.
Ich bin	zu meiner Freundin zu meinem Freund in die Disko	gegangen.
	zu Hause	geblieben.

IM JULI

Im Juli bin ich zu vielen Partys gegangen. Bei einer Party habe ich Omri kennen gelernt.

Hast du die Betti kennen gelernt?

Hör zu und lies die Bildgeschichte.

Treff-spezial-Ferien

Lies die Annoncen und sieh dir die Bilder an. Was passt wozu?

Beispiel

1 *B*

TREFF-SPEZIAL-FERIEN

1

Gesucht: Der Junge aus Marburg, der am 27. Jan. in Koblenz am Bahnhof war und mir zulachte. Du hast mittellange, hellbraune Haare und hast eine schwarze Lederjacke getragen. Bitte schreib an Annette Brand, Strandweg 12, 3500 Burgdorf, Schweiz. Ich warte!

2

Hallo, Asaf! Wir haben uns auf dem Campingplatz Waldruh im Schwarzwald kennen gelernt. Ich habe sehr kurze, blonde Haare und heiße Birgit. Schicke deinen Brief an: Birgit Neumeyer, Bahnhofstraße 44, 7901 Bernstadt.

3

Wo seid ihr? Die zwei schönen Mädchen aus Österreich, die am 12. Juli in der Disko in Korfu mit uns getanzt haben? Thomas u. Oliver denken noch an Euch! Ruft an unter 02 14/2 75 77.

4

Wo ist das Girl, das am 14. Juni um 13 Uhr im Gasthaus ‚Alpenhof' mit mir einen Milkshake getrunken hat? Du hast eine dunkelblaue Hose, einen rot-weiß-blauen Pulli und rote Schuhe getragen und hast blonde, schulterlange Haare. Bitte ruf mich an – dein Thorsten. Telefon: 0 98/05 831.

5

Der Junge mit dem Spaniel sucht das Mädchen mit dem Schäferhund. Du warst am 19. u. 21. August im Jenischpark. Bitte melde dich bei Mathias Linden, Eichendorffstr. 10, 22587 Hamburg.

6

SOS Knut! Du warst in der Zeit vom 20. Juli bis 3. August auf Menorca im Hotel ‚Plaza Mayor'. Du hast dunkelblonde Haare und bist sehr groß. Ich bin das Mädchen mit dem Strohhut! Bitte melde dich bei Katrin Wolfinger, Kropacher Weg 2, 35398 Gießen - heute!

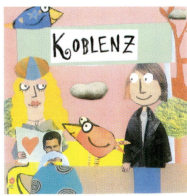

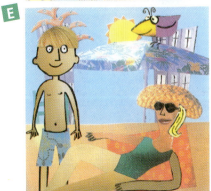

Schreib eine Annonce wie diese und zeichne ein passendes Bild dazu.

IM OKTOBER

Wie ist Lars zum Schwimmbad gekommen?

Sieh dir die Bilder an und schreib Sätze auf.

Beispiel
Lars ist mit dem Rad zum Schwimmbad gekommen.

Im Oktober habe ich eine Klassenfahrt nach England gemacht.

Sandra

Lars

Michael

Thomas

Francesca

Martina

Ich bin gut angekommen

Lies die Postkarten.

Hallo Raphael!
Das Wetter hier ist fantastisch! Viel wärmer als in Deutschland. Wir sind um 19 Uhr in Liverpool angekommen – der IC-Zug aus London hatte eine Stunde Verspätung.
Dein Michael

Raphael Ziegert
Passauer Str. 10
84076 Pfeffenhausen
Germany

Liebe Anja!
Ich bin gut angekommen. Die Reise war aber lang. Wir sind mit dem Bus von Harwich nach London gefahren und dann weiter mit dem Zug nach Manchester. Das ist eine sehr schöne Stadt.
Viele Grüße
Deine Dorit

Anja Stegemann
Hamburger Str. 25
25421 Pinneberg
GERMANY

Richtig oder falsch?

1 Michael hat eine Karte an Raphael geschrieben.
2 Dorit hat eine Karte von Anja bekommen.
3 Dorits Reise war sehr lang.
4 Anja ist mit dem Bus von Harwich nach London gefahren.
5 Michael ist um sieben Uhr abends in Liverpool angekommen.
6 Michaels Zug ist pünktlich angekommen.
7 Dorit ist mit dem Bus nach Manchester gefahren.

Tipp des Tages

Wie	bist du ist er	nach London zum Schwimmbad	gefahren? gekommen?

Ich bin Er ist Sie ist	mit dem Rad mit dem Zug mit dem Auto	gekommen. gefahren.
	um sieben Uhr	angekommen.

Wie war die Reise?		
Die Fahrt Die Reise	war	gut. lang.
Wir	waren	seekrank.

Kannst du einen Satz bilden?

Beispiel
1 *Er hat Brötchen und Kuchen gekauft.*

 Wie ist es richtig?

Schreib die Sätze richtig auf.

Lieber Kurt!

Auf Janes Brief ist Schokolade gefallen. Schreib den Brief noch einmal. Füll die Lücken mit den Wörtern unten aus.

stürmisch
geschlafen
müde
gegessen
bin
angekommen
war
geschmeckt
seekrank
gekommen

Lieber Kurt!

Ich bin gut nach Hause ▬▬▬. Ich habe im Zug ▬▬▬, dann habe ich im Speisewagen ▬▬▬ das Essen hat mir aber nicht gut ▬▬▬ Die Überfahrt von Hamburg nach Harwich ▬▬▬ fürchterlich. Die Nordsee war ▬▬▬, und ich war ▬▬▬. Ich ▬▬ um 16 Uhr in Harwich ▬▬▬. Natürlich war ich sehr ▬▬▬, aber jetzt geht es mir wieder besser.

Schreib bald wieder
Deine Jane

Wo ist das Ende?

Finde das Ende zu jedem Satz.

Beispiel

1 *Ich habe eine Pizza gegessen.*

1 Ich habe eine Pizza ...	**6** Ich habe ein Glas Milch ...
2 Ich bin zu einer Party ...	**7** Ich habe ein neues Fahrrad ...
3 Ich habe einen Film ...	**8** Ich habe Tennis ...
4 Ich habe Jeans ...	**9** Ich bin mit der Straßenbahn ...
5 Ich habe eine Party ...	**10** Ich bin nach Amerika ...

getrunken   gegangen

gesehen   gegessen

gefahren   gegeben

geflogen   bekommen

getragen   gespielt

 Lieber Karl-Heinz!

Lies die Postkarten und beantworte die Fragen.

Lieber Karl-Heinz!
Hier ist das Wetter viel besser als zu Hause. Jeden Tag Sonne! Ich bin gestern im „Tower of London" gewesen, vorgestern in Windsor. Wir haben abends Tennis gespielt oder sind zu Hause geblieben und haben etwas ferngesehen. Ich habe heute ein sehr nettes englisches Mädchen kennen gelernt – lange Haare und blau-grüne Augen. Ich gehe mit ihr morgen Abend in die Disko. Ich habe leider nur noch 3 Tage, dann muss ich nach Hause kommen. So ein Pech! Also, bis dann,
Axel

Karl-Heinz Gerlach
Werfelstr. 19
12305 Berlin

Germany

1 Wer hat an Karl-Heinz geschrieben?

2 Wer war in London?

3 Wo ist Claudia?

4 Was hat Axel abends gemacht?

5 Wie sieht Axels englische Freundin aus?

6 Wohin ist Claudia gestern gegangen?

7 Was hat sie getrunken?

8 Wie lange bleibt Axel noch in England?

Lieber Karl-Heinz!
Nur noch 3 Tage, dann bin ich wieder bei dir! Die Leute hier in Swansea sind alle sehr nett. Ich bin viel weggegangen und habe viel Englisch gesprochen. Gestern bin ich sogar zu einer Party gegangen – aber mach dir keine Sorgen, ich habe keinen tollen Engländer kennen gelernt. Ich habe nur ein Glas Bier getrunken und gar nicht getanzt.
Ich vermisse dich so!
Deine Claudia x

Karl-Heinz Gerlach
Werfelstr. 19
12305 Berlin

Germany.

1 Asking questions about events in the past

Was hast du	heute im Mai gestern Abend an deinem Geburtstag letztes Jahr am Mittwoch	gemacht?	What did you do	today? in May? yesterday evening? on your birthday? last year? on Wednesday?

Was hast du gekauft?	What have you bought?
Was hast du zum Geburtstag bekommen?	What did you get for your birthday?
Wie bist du gefahren?	How did you travel?

2 How to talk about things you have done

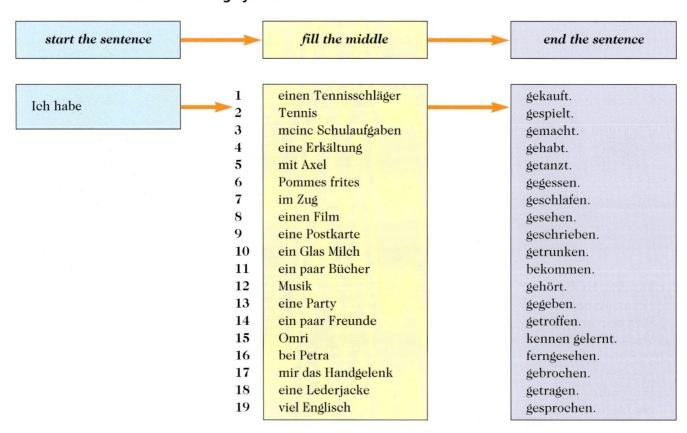

start the sentence	fill the middle	end the sentence
Ich habe	1 einen Tennisschläger 2 Tennis 3 meine Schulaufgaben 4 eine Erkältung 5 mit Axel 6 Pommes frites 7 im Zug 8 einen Film 9 eine Postkarte 10 ein Glas Milch 11 ein paar Bücher 12 Musik 13 eine Party 14 ein paar Freunde 15 Omri 16 bei Petra 17 mir das Handgelenk 18 eine Lederjacke 19 viel Englisch	gekauft. gespielt. gemacht. gehabt. getanzt. gegessen. geschlafen. gesehen. geschrieben. getrunken. bekommen. gehört. gegeben. getroffen. kennen gelernt. ferngesehen. gebrochen. getragen. gesprochen.

1 *I bought a tennis racquet.*
2 *I played tennis.*
3 *I did my homework.*
4 *I had a cold.*
5 *I danced with Axel.*
6 *I ate chips.*
7 *I slept in the train.*

8 *I saw a film.*
9 *I wrote a postcard.*
10 *I drank a glass of milk.*
11 *I got a few books.*
12 *I listened to some music.*
13 *I gave a party.*
14 *I met a few friends.*

15 *I met/got to know Omri.*
16 *I watched television at Petra's house.*
17 *I broke my wrist.*
18 *I wore a leather jacket.*
19 *I spoke a lot of English.*

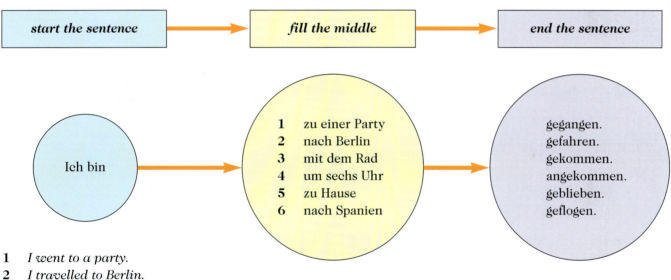

1 *I went to a party.*
2 *I travelled to Berlin.*
3 *I came by bike.*
4 *I arrived at six o'clock.*
5 *I stayed at home.*
6 *I flew to Spain.*

3 Describing events in the past

Die Fahrt mit der Bahn		ganz gut.	*The train journey was quite good.*
Die See	war	stürmisch.	*The sea was rough.*
Die Reise		lang.	*The journey was long.*
Wir	waren	seekrank.	*We were seasick.*

Spelling

1a   Capitals

All nouns begin with a capital letter (not only the words which start a sentence):

Was isst du zum **F**rühstück? **B**rötchen und **M**armelade.	What do you eat for breakfast? Rolls and jam.

1b   Small letters

Adjectives are always written with small letters even if they refer to nationalities:

Isst du gern **d**eutsches Brot? Das ist ein **e**nglisches Auto.	Do you like (eating) German bread? That's an English car.

Exception:
Adjectives that refer to nationalities or colours and have a preposition in front
are written with capital letters:

Sie sagt es **auf D**eutsch Er trägt dasselbe Hemd **in G**rün	She says it in German. He wears the same shirt in green.

1c   ss/ß

Use **ß** only when you are sure it is correct. If not, it is safer to write **ss**.

Use **ß**	after a long vowel	Grü**ß**e	
Use **ss**	after a short vowel	Ku**ss**	Viele süße Grüße und Küsse!

Numbers and quantities

2a   Cardinal numbers

1	eins	11	elf	21	einundzwanzig	100	hundert
2	zwei/zwo	12	zwölf	22	zweiundzwanzig	101	hunderteins
3	drei	13	dreizehn	29	neunundzwanzig	102	hundertzwei
4	vier	14	vierzehn	30	dreißig	199	hundertneunundneunzig
5	fünf	15	fünfzehn	40	vierzig	200	zweihundert
6	sechs	16	sechzehn	50	fünfzig	999	neunhundertneunundneunzig
7	sieben	17	siebzehn	60	sechzig		
8	acht	18	achtzehn	70	siebzig	1 000	tausend
9	neun	19	neunzehn	80	achtzig	1 000 000	eine Million
10	zehn	20	zwanzig	90	neunzig	2 000 000	zwei Millionen

Zwanzig Minuten mit dem Bus. Das ist die Linie dreiundvierzig.	Twenty minutes by bus. That's bus route 43.

2b   Ordinal numbers

These words are to say first, second, etc. For most numbers up to **19th** you just add -te (or -ten).

Exceptions:	**1st** erste(n)	**3rd** dritte(n)	**7th** siebte(n)	**8th** achte(n)

From **20th** onwards you add -ste (or -sten).

Die ers**te** Stunde.	The first lesson.
Am zwanzig**sten** März.	On the twentieth of March.
Die zwei**te** Straße links.	The second street on the left.
Die **dritte** Straße rechts.	The third street on the right.
Die Kassetten sind im **ersten** Stock.	Cassettes are on the first floor.
Das ist im vier**ten** Stock.	It's on the fourth floor.

(See also section **8**.)

2c Weights, measures and containers

Hundert Gramm Wurst.	A hundred grammes of sausage.
Dreihundert Gramm Käse.	Three hundred grammes of cheese.
Ein Pfund Tomaten.	A pound of tomatoes.
Ein Kilo Bananen.	A kilo of bananas.
Anderthalb Kilo Äpfel.	One and a half kilos of apples.
Ein Liter Milch.	A litre of milk.
Ein halber Liter Wasser.	Half a litre of water.
Ein Glas Honig.	A jar of honey.
Ein Stück Seife.	A bar of soap.
Ein Becher Margarine.	A tub of margarine.
Eine Schachtel Pralinen.	A box of chocolates.
Eine Tube Zahnpasta.	A tube of toothpaste.
Eine Packung Kekse.	A packet of biscuits.
Eine Dose Tomatensuppe.	A tin of tomato soup.
Eine Flasche Milch.	A bottle of milk.

Addressing people

3a Greetings

The following greetings are normally used amongst friends:

Hallo!
Grüß dich!
Grüßt euch! *(for more than one)*
Wie geht's?

More formal greetings are:

Guten Morgen! *or* Morgen!	**7.00**
Guten Tag!	
Guten Abend!	**18.00**
Guten Appetit!	At mealtimes

3b Farewells

Tschüss!	*(to friends)*
(Auf) Wiedersehen!	*(more formal)*
(Auf) Wiederhören!	*(on the telephone)*
Gute Nacht, schlaf gut!	*(when going to bed)*

3c Ways of saying you'll see someone again

bis	eins / halb zwei / neun Uhr		at		one (o'clock) / one thirty / nine (o'clock)
	morgen / Samstagabend / Freitagvormittag		(I'll) see you		tomorrow / on Saturday evening / on Friday morning
	nächste	Woche		next	week
	nächsten	Monat / Samstag		next	month / Saturday
bis	nächstes	Jahr / Mal		next	year / time
	heute Abend			this evening	
	bald			soon	

3d Letters

Begin	Liebe Gabi!	Dear Gabi
	Lieber Peter!	Dear Peter
End	Herzliche Grüße	Best wishes
	Herzliche Grüße und Küsse	Best wishes and kisses
	Schreib bald wieder!	Write again soon!
	Dein Michael	Yours, Michael
	Deine Rachel	Yours, Rachel

Questions

4a Ordinary questions

Ordinary questions can be asked in the same way as in English by beginning with the verb, e.g. Have you …? Do you …? Can you …?

Haben Sie einen Stadtplan?	Have you got a town map?
Ist hier eine Bank in der Nähe?	Is there a bank nearby?
Hast du Lust, ins Kino zu gehen?	Do you want to go to the cinema?
Kommst du mit?	Are you coming?

4b Question words

Most other questions begin with a **'question word'**:

Wie? *(usually: How?)*

Wie findest du deine Stadt?	What do you think of your town?
Wie kommst du zur Party?	How are you getting to the party?
Wie kommen wir dorthin?	How are we getting there?

Wer? *(Who?)*

Wer kommt mit zur Party?	Who's coming with us to the party?
Wer ist Belli?	Who is Betti?

Was? *(What?)*

Was gibt es hier zu sehen?	What's there to see here?
Was hältst du von Asla?	What do you think of Asla?
Was kostet ein Brief nach England?	What does it cost to send a letter to England?

Wann? *(When?)*

Wann kommt der Zug an?	When does the train arrive?
Wann fährt der nächste Zug nach Bonn?	When does the next train to Bonn leave?

Wo? *(Where?)*

Wo ist hier die Post?	Where is the post office?
Wo kauft man das?	Where can you buy that?
Wo kann ich hier Schuhe bekommen?	Where can I find the shoe section?

Wohin? *(Where to?)*

Wohin fahren wir?	Where are we going?

Wofür? *(On what?)*

Wofür gibst du dein Geld aus?	What do you spend your money on?

Wie viel? *(How many? How much?)*

Wie viel ist das?	How much is that?
Wie viel willst du ausgeben?	How much do you want to spend?

Um wie viel Uhr? *(At what time?)*

Um wie viel Uhr isst du dein Mittagessen?	When do you have lunch?

Welche(r/s)? *(Which …?)*

Welche Linie ist das?	What route is that?
Welches Bild ist das?	Which picture is it?
Von **welchem** Gleis fährt der Zug nach Ulm?	What platform does the train to Ulm leave from?

Warum? *(Why?)*

Warum (nicht)?	Why (not)?
Warum kommst du nicht mit?	Why aren't you coming?

Days of the week

5a   What day is it?

Was ist heute für ein Tag?		What day is it today?	
Heute ist	Montag. Dienstag. Mittwoch. Donnerstag. Freitag. Samstag. Sonntag.	Today is	Monday. Tuesday. Wednesday. Thursday. Friday. Saturday. Sunday.

5b   The day and part of the day

Montag Dienstag Mittwoch	-vormittag -nachmittag -abend	morning afternoon evening

5c   On (plus the day of the week and part of the day)

am	Montag Dienstag Mittwoch	-vormittag -nachmittag -abend	on Monday morning on Tuesday afternoon on Wednesday evening

5d   Regularly on the same day

montags dienstags freitags	on Mondays on Tuesdays on Fridays

Notice that these begin with a small letter.

Months of the year

6a   die Monate

Januar	Juli
Februar	August
März	September
April	Oktober
Mai	November
Juni	Dezember

6b   In + month

Im	Januar Juni September Dezember	In	January June September December

The seasons

7a   die Jahreszeiten

der Sommer	summer
der Herbst	autumn
der Winter	winter
der Frühling	spring

7b   In + season

Im	Sommer Herbst Winter Frühling	In the	summer autumn winter spring

The date

8a   What's the date today?

Den Wievielten haben wir heute?			What's the date today?	
Wir haben den	ersten zweiten dritten vierten zehnten zwanzigsten einundzwanzigsten dreißigsten einunddreißigsten	Januar. Februar. April. Mai. Juli. August. Oktober. November. Dezember.	It's the	first of January. second of February. third of April. fourth of May. tenth of July. twentieth of August. twenty-first of October. thirtieth of November. thirty-first of December.

(See also section **2b**.)

8b   On … + date

am	ersten (1.)	Januar	on the	first of January
	dritten (3.)	Februar		third of February
	vierten (4.)	April		fourth of April
	zehnten (10.)	Juni		tenth of July
	neunzehnten (19.)	August		nineteenth of August
	zwanzigsten (20.)	November		twentieth of November

8c   Dates on letters

den	1sten	20sten	Januar
	2ten	27sten	Februar
	3ten	28sten	April
	4ten	30sten	Oktober
	18ten	31sten	Dezember

Oktober	Berlin,	den 20sten

Time

9a   What time is it?

| Wie viel Uhr ist es? |
| Wie spät ist es? |

| What time is it? |

9b   On the hour

Es ist	eins.	or	Es ist	ein	Uhr
	zwei.			zwei	
	drei.			drei	
Um	vier.		Um	vier	

It's	1	o'clock
	2	
	3	
At	4	

9c   Quarter to/past the hour

Es ist	Viertel	vor	eins
			zwei.
			drei.
Um		nach	vier.

It's	a quarter	to	1
			2
			3
At		past	4

9d   Half past the hour

Es ist	halb	eins.
		zwei.
Um		drei.

It's	half past	12
		1
At		2

Note: Um halb **drei** = at 2.30, i.e. halfway to 3.00.

9e   Minutes to/past the hour (5, 10, 20, 25)

Es ist	fünf	vor	eins.
	zehn		zwei.
	zwanzig		drei.
Um	fünfundzwanzig	nach	vier.

It's	5	to	1
	10		2
	20		3
At	25	past	4

Other minutes (7, 9, 14, 19 etc.)

Es ist	sieben	Minuten	vor	eins.
	neun			zwei.
	vierzehn			drei.
Um	neunzehn		nach	vier.

It's	7	minutes	to	1
	9			2
	14			3
At	19		past	4

9f   Midday/midnight

Es ist	zwölf Uhr.
	Mittag.
Um	Mitternacht

It's	12 o'clock
	midday
At	midnight

Note also the following way of saying you are doing something 'at midday/midnight':

| Zu | Mittag. |
| | Mitternacht. |

Du, ihr, Sie

All three of these words are translated by 'you'. They are used as follows:

10a   *du*

Speaking to a young person

– Wie heißt du? – Dominik. – Wie alt bist du? – Acht.	*What's your name?* *Dominik.* *How old are you?* *Eight.*

Between friends old or young *(people you usually call by their first name)*

– Kommst du mit ins Kino? – Ja, gern.	*Are you coming to the cinema?* *Yes, I'd like to.*

In the family

– Vati, kommst du mit in die Stadt? – Nein, ich bleibe zu Hause.	*Dad, are you coming into town?* *No, I'm staying at home.*
– Kannst du mir mal helfen, Mutti? – Ja, Moment.	*Can you help me, mum?* *Yes, wait a minute.*

10b   *ihr*

Speaking to young people

Jens – Was macht ihr heute? Alexa und Tobias – Wir gehen schwimmen.	*What are you doing today?* *We're going swimming.*
Lehrer – Was macht ihr da alle?	*What are you all doing?*

Speaking to friends or relatives

Ute – Mutti und Vati, geht ihr heute Abend ins Kino?	*Mum and dad, are you going to the cinema tonight?*
Paul – Oma, Opa, kommt ihr zu meinem Geburtstag?	*Grandma and grandpa, are you coming to my birthday?*

10c   *Sie*

Talking to one or more adults *(other than close friends or relatives)*

– Wo wohnen Sie? – Wie heißen Sie?	*Where do you live?* *What's your name?*

Verbs

11a   **The infinitive**

*In the vocabulary list, verbs are listed in the **infinitive**.*
*The infinitive ending is **-en**.*
This is the part of the word which means 'to', for example 'to eat', 'to do', etc.

wohn**en** heiß**en** ess**en**	*to live* *to be called* *to eat*

*(See also sections **11n**, **11o**, **11p** and **18c**.)*

11b   **Present Tense (regular verbs)**

*Verbs which follow the usual pattern are called **regular verbs**.*

11c   **Talking about yourself (I): ich**

*The verb ending that goes with **ich** is **-e**:*

Ich heiß**e** Kurt Meier. **Ich** wohn**e** in München.	*My name is …* *I live in …*

*(For **ich bin**, **ich muss**, **ich will** etc. see section **11j - n**.)*

11d Talking to other people (you)

Address one friend or young person as du

The verb ending that goes with **du** is **-st**:

Wo wohn**st** du?	*Where do you live?*
Was mein**st** du?	*What do you mean?*

Verbs with an s-sound before endings just add a **-t**:

Wie heiß**t** **du**?	*What's your name?*
Was lies**t** **du**?	*What are you reading?*

Address more than one friend or young people as ihr

The verb ending that goes with **ihr** is **-t**:

Wo wohn**t** **ihr**?	*Where do you live?*
Was ess**t** **ihr**?	*What are you eating?*

Address one or more adults as Sie

(**Sie** *with a capital* **S***!*) The verb ending that goes with **Sie** is **-en**:

Wo wohn**en** **Sie**?	*Where do you live?*
Wie heiß**en** **Sie**?	*What is your name?*

11e Talking about somebody or something (he/she/it/one): er/sie/es/man

The verb ending that goes with **er/sie/es/man,** or with a name, is **-t**:

Mein Onkel wohn**t** in Wien.	*My uncle lives in …*
Er heiß**t** Kurt.	*His name is …*
Frau Meier wohn**t** in Österreich.	*Mrs Meier lives in …*
Sie heiß**t** Erika.	*Her name is …*
Mein Meerschweinchen heiß**t** Amanda.	*My guinea pig is called Amanda.*
Es trink**t** Milch.	*It drinks milk.*
Man kauf**t** Brot in der Bäckerei.	*You buy bread at the baker's.*

11f Talking about yourself and others (we): wir

The verb ending that goes with **wir** is **-en**:

Wir wohn**en** in Köln.	*We live in Cologne.*
Wir ess**en** Brot mit Wurst.	*We eat bread with sausage.*
Meine Schwester und ich trink**en** Kaffee.	*My sister and I drink coffee.*

11g Talking about others or things (they): sie

(**Sie** *with a small* **s***!*) The ending that goes with **sie** is **-en**:

Die Häuser steh**en** am Stadtrand.	*The houses are on the outskirts of town.*
Sie steh**en** am Stadtrand.	*They are on the outskirts of town.*
Die Meiers wohn**en** in Österreich.	*The Meiers live in Austria.*
Die Jungen heiß**en** Peter und Michael.	*The boys are called Peter and Michael.*
Sie trink**en** Milch.	*They drink milk.*

11h Regular verb endings at a glance

Look again at sections **11b - 11g**. Here is the complete pattern of endings for regular verbs:

Infinitive: **wohn en** *(**to** live)*

ich	-e	Ich **wohne** in Hamburg.	*I live/am living in Hamburg.*
du	-st	**Wohnst** du in Berlin?	*Do you live in Berlin?*
er / sie / es / man	-t	Sie **wohnt** hier.	*She lives here.*
wir	-en	Wir **wohnen** in Leeds.	*We live/are living in Leeds.*
ihr	-t	**Wohnt** ihr in Deutschland?	*Do you live in Germany?*
Sie	-en	**Wohnen** Sie in der Schweiz?	*Do you live in Switzerland?*
sie	-en	Sie **wohnen** in der Stadtmitte.	*They live in the town centre.*

Note:	Sie	=	*you*
	sie	=	*they*

11i Irregular changes affecting some verbs

*Sometimes the main vowel in the infinitive changes, but only affects the **du** and **er/sie/es** parts of the verb:*

essen	du **i**sst er **i**sst	**e - i**	*you eat* *he eats*
spr**e**chen	du spr**i**chst man spr**i**cht		*you speak* *one speaks/they speak*
l**e**sen	du l**ie**st sie l**ie**st	**e - ie**	*you read* *she reads*
s**e**hen	du s**ie**hst er s**ie**ht		*you see* *he sees*
schl**a**fen	du schl**ä**fst er schl**ä**ft	**a - ä**	*you sleep* *he sleeps*
tr**a**gen	du tr**ä**gst sie tr**ä**gt		*you wear* *she wears*

11j Some special verbs

Some very common verbs, which are used very frequently, are irregular
(i.e. they don't follow the normal pattern), and should be learnt separately.

11k haben (to have) *Just two forms are not regular:*

Hast du ein Haustier? Tante Liesel **hat** ein Reihenhaus.	du **hast** ... er/sie/es **hat** ...	*you have ...* *he/she/it has ...*

11l sein (to be) *All the parts of this verb are irregular:*

Ich bin 13 Jahre alt.	ich **bin**	*I am*
Wer **bist du**?	du **bist**	*you are*
Er ist 15 Jahre alt.	er	*he is*
Sie ist sehr groß.	sie	*she is*
Es ist schön hier.	es } **ist**	*it is*
Man ist Deutscher.	man	*one is/they are/you are*
Maria und ich sind Geschwister.	wir **sind**	*we are*
Seid ihr alle da?	ihr **seid**	*you are*
Wer **sind Sie**?	Sie **sind**	*you are*
Veronica und Kirsten sind in der Schule.	sie **sind**	*they are*

11m wissen (to know) *Three parts of this verb are irregular:*

Ich weiß nicht. **Weißt du** das? **Sie weiß** nicht.	*I don't know.* *Do you know that?* *She doesn't know.*	ich **weiß** du **weißt** er/sie/es **weiß**	*I know* *you know* *he/she/it knows*

11n Modal verbs

This is the name given to the following group of verbs:

	können *(can)*	**müssen** *(must, have to)*	**wollen** *(want to)*	**sollen** *(should)*	**dürfen** *(allowed to)*
ich	kann	muss	will	soll	darf
du	kannst	musst	willst	sollst	darfst
er/sie/es/man	kann	muss	will	soll	darf
wir	können	müssen	wollen	sollen	dürfen
ihr	könnt	müsst	wollt	sollt	dürft
Sie	können	müssen	wollen	sollen	dürfen
sie	können	müssen	wollen	sollen	dürfen

*These verbs usually lead to **another verb**, at the end of the clause, which is in the infinitive:*

Ich **kann** nicht in die Schule **gehen**. Ich **muss** zu Hause **bleiben**. Wir **wollen** zwei Nächte **bleiben**. Du **sollst** diese Tabletten **nehmen**. Ich **darf** keinen Käse **essen**.	*I can't go to school.* *I have to stay at home.* *We want to stay for two nights.* *You should take these tablets.* *I'm not allowed to eat cheese.*

*Note that there is no need to write **zu** before the verbs which follow modal verbs, unlike in section **11p**.*

11o Would like ...

Use the following to express 'would like' in German. The verb used (**mögen**) is also a modal verb, although it is not in the Present Tense here:

ich	möchte	I would like
du	möchtest	you would like
er/sie/es/man	möchte	he/she/it/one would like
wir	möchten	we would like
ihr	möchtet	you would like
Sie	möchten	you would like
sie	möchten	they would like

Ich **möchte** eine Hotelliste, bitte.	I would like a list of hotels, please.
Möchten Sie auch einen Stadtplan?	Would you like a town map as well?
Möchtest du ein Eis essen?	Would you like an ice cream?

11p Zu + an infinitive

The infinitive of a verb means 'to ...', but sometimes an extra **zu** appears before it:

Was gibt es in der Stadt **zu sehen**?	What is there **to see** in the town?
Noch etwas **zu trinken**?	Anything else **to drink**?
Hast du Lust, Tennis **zu spielen**?	Would you like **to play** tennis?

11q Commands

There are three main ways of giving commands in German:

Talking to a friend, or the teacher talking to one student	Talking to two or more friends, or the teacher talking to two or more students	Talking to adults, teachers, officials, shopkeepers	
Komm 'rein.	Kommt 'rein.	Kommen Sie herein.	Come in.
Setz dich.	Setzt euch.	Setzen Sie sich.	Sit down.
Schlag das Buch auf.	Schlagt das Buch auf.	Schlagen Sie das Buch auf.	Open the book.
Hör gut zu.	Hört gut zu.	Hören Sie gut zu.	Listen carefully.
Mach weiter.	Macht weiter.	Machen Sie weiter.	Continue working now.
Schreib es auf.	Schreibt es auf.	Schreiben Sie es auf.	Write it down.
Trag die Tabelle ein.	Tragt die Tabelle ein.	Tragen Sie die Tabelle ein.	Copy the chart.
Lies die Namen.	Lest die Namen.	Lesen Sie die Namen.	Read the names.
Schau auf die Karte.	Schaut auf die Karte.	Schauen Sie auf die Karte.	Look at the map.
Füll die Lücken aus.	Füllt die Lücken aus.	Füllen Sie die Lücken aus.	Fill in the gaps.

Note that sometimes these may be followed by an exclamation mark, e.g. **Komm 'rein!**

11r Reflexive verbs

These verbs require an extra (reflexive) pronoun, and are called 'reflexive' because the action 'reflects back' on the doer:

Ich wasche **mich** um sieben Uhr.	I have a wash at 7.00. (i.e. **I** wash **myself** ...)

11s Separable verbs

Some verbs include a prefix, which separates from the main part of the verb and is placed at the end of the clause.
Some examples of separable verbs are **auf**stehen, **aus**fallen, **fern**sehen.

Ich **stehe** um halb sieben **auf**.	I get up at half past six.
Wie **sieht** Anke **aus**?	What does Anke look like?
Sieh dir die Bilder **an**.	Look at the pictures.

11t   The Future Tense

The simplest way of talking about the future in German is to use the
Present Tense of the verb with a word or phrase to indicate the future:

Time marker	Present Tense	
Morgen	**fahre ich** nach Frankfurt.	Tomorrow I'm going to Frankfurt.
Nächste Woche	**gehe ich** schwimmen.	I'm going swimming next week.
Am Montag	**besuche** ich meine Großeltern.	I'm visiting my grandparents on Monday.
Dieses Jahr	**fahren wir** auf einen Campingplatz.	We're going to a campsite this year.

11u   The Perfect Tense

This is the most common tense used in German to express events which have happened in the past. There are
two parts to the Perfect Tense – the **auxiliary verb**, which is always a part of the Present Tense of either **haben**
or **sein**, and the **past participle** of the verb, which goes to the end of the sentence.

Most verbs form the Perfect Tense with **haben**. The past participle of most verbs is formed by adding **ge-** to the
er/sie/es part of the Present Tense.

Ich **habe** eine Klassenfahrt **gemacht**.	I went on a class trip.
Sie **hat** eine Kassette **gekauft**.	She bought a cassette.
Wir **haben** Tennis **gespielt**.	We played tennis.

Several verbs have past participles which are not formed in the same way and are therefore called **irregular**.
These are shown in verb tables, and you should learn them by heart. Some you have met include:

Ich **habe** einen Job **bekommen**.	I got a job.
Axel **hat** eine Party **gegeben**.	Axel had a party.
Er **hat** sehr lange **geschlafen**.	He slept for a long time.
Wir **haben** Tee **getrunken**.	We drank tea.
Sie **haben** den neuen Film **gesehen**.	They have seen the new film.
Habt ihr die Postkarten **geschrieben**?	Have you written the postcards?
Hast du deine Freundin **getroffen**?	Did you meet your friend?
Sie **hat** das Handgelenk **gebrochen**.	She broke her wrist.

Some verbs form the Perfect Tense with **sein**, usually verbs of movement or travel. The past participles of these
verbs are also **irregular**. Some you have met include:

Ich **bin** mit dem Rad **gekommen**.	I came by bike.
Wie **bist** du **gefahren**?	How did you travel?
Wir **sind** um sieben Uhr nach Hause **angekommen**.	We arrived home at seven o'clock.
Ilse **ist** zu einer Party **gegangen**.	Ilse has gone to a party.
Sie **sind** zu Hause **geblieben**.	They stayed at home.
Er **ist** nach Amerika **geflogen**.	He has flown to America.

11v   Was/had

Note also:

Die Reise **war** lang.	The journey was long.
Wir **waren** seekrank.	We were seasick.
Der Zug **hatte** Verspätung.	The train was late.
Anne **hatte** Kopfschmerzen.	Anne had a headache.

Negatives

12a   kein

kein (no, not a) **is used before a noun.** It changes its endings like **ein**. (See sections **14** and **17d**):

Ich habe	**keinen** Hund.	I haven't got a dog.
Hast du	**keine** Katze?	Have you got a cat?
Sie hat	**kein** Haustier.	She has no pets.
Sie haben	**keine** Geschwister.	They have no brothers and sisters.

12b nicht

nicht *(not)* *is used in other situations:*

Ich spiele **nicht** gern Tennis.	*I don't like playing tennis.*
Ich esse **nicht** gern Schokolade.	*I don't like eating chocolate.*
Er kommt **nicht** mit ins Kino.	*He isn't coming with us to the cinema.*
Sie geht **nicht** in die Stadt.	*She isn't going into town.*

12c nichts

nichts *(nothing/not anything)*

Ich trinke **nichts** zum Frühstück.	*I don't drink anything for breakfast.*

Nouns

13a Writing nouns

Remember that nouns are **always** *written with a capital letter.*

13b Genders: The three groups of nouns

M	F	N
der Hund	**die** Katze	**das** Pferd
(the dog)	*(the cat)*	*(the horse)*

English has one article (one word for 'the') for all nouns, but German nouns have either **der, die** *or* **das**. *These are called 'masculine' (**M**), 'feminine' (**F**) and 'neuter' (**N**).*

Note also the words for 'a':

M	F	N
ein Hund	**eine** Katze	**ein** Pferd
(a dog)	*(a cat)*	*(a horse)*

13c Plurals: Talking about more than one person, thing etc.

Nouns change in various ways in the plural, but **der, die, das** *all become* **die:**

SINGULAR	der	die	das
PLURAL		**die**	

The plurals are usually shown in the vocabulary list in the following way:

der	Hund(e)	**(e)**	*means that the plural is (die) Hund**e***
die	Katze(n)	**(n)**	*means that the plural is (die) Katze**n***
das	Haus(¨er)	**(¨er)**	*means that the plural is (die) H**ä**us**er***
das	Zimmer(–)	**(–)**	*means that the plural stays the same: (die) Zimmer*

Although there are many exceptions, the following rules of thumb will prove helpful when you need to form the plural of nouns:

Many masculine plural nouns end in -e:

Hund	*dog*		Hund**e**	*dogs*
Freund	*friend*		Freund**e**	*friends*

Many neuter plural nouns end in -e or ¨-er:

Heft	*exercise book*		Heft**e**	*exercise books*
Haus	*house*		H**ä**us**er**	*houses*

A large number of feminine plural nouns end in -n or -en:

Katze	*cat*		Katz**en**	*cats*
Straße	*street*		Straß**en**	*streets*
Schwester	*sister*		Schwester**n**	*sisters*
Wohnung	*flat*		Wohnung**en**	*flats*

13d   Some nouns have different masculine and feminine forms:

M	F	
Arzt	Ärztin	doctor
Freund	Freundin	friend
Partner	Partnerin	partner
Sänger	Sängerin	singer
Schüler	Schülerin	pupil
Student	Studentin	student
Verkäufer	Verkäuferin	sales assistant

13e   Nationalities

There are different masculine and feminine forms here, too:

M		F	
Engländer	*English man*	Engländerin	*English woman*
Österreicher	*Austrian man*	Österreicherin	*Austrian woman*
Schweizer	*Swiss man*	Schweizerin	*Swiss woman*
Italiener	*Italian man*	Italienerin	*Italian woman*
Deutscher	*German man*	Deutsche	*German woman*
Ire	*Irish man*	Irin	*Irish woman*
Schotte	*Scottish man*	Schottin	*Scottish woman*
Franzose	*French man*	Französin	*French woman*

13f   Compound nouns

Sometimes two (or more) nouns join together to form a new noun, called a compound noun.
The gender (M, F or N) is decided by the second (or last) noun:

Stadt + **der** Plan	**der** Stadtplan	*street plan*
Haupt + **die** Post	**die** Hauptpost	*main post office*
Kranken + **das** Haus	**das** Krankenhaus	*hospital*
Jahr + **der** Markt	**der** Jahrmarkt	*fair*
Fuß + Gänger + **die** Zone	**die** Fußgängerzone	*pedestrian precinct*

Note how compound nouns, like all other nouns, have only one capital letter.

Cases

14a   The Cases

When articles (words for 'the' and 'a') change, nouns are said to be in different cases. You can see from the illustrations here how important it can be to put articles in the correct cases!

– Was, die Katze frisst   *What, the cat is eating*
den Wellensittich?   *the budgie?*
– Nein, **der** Hund.   *No, the dog (is eating the budgie).*

– Was, die Katze frisst   *What, the cat is eating*
den Wellensittich?   *the budgie?*
– Nein, **den** Goldfisch.   *No, (the cat is eating) the goldfish.*

14b The Nominative case

In dictionaries and glossaries nouns always appear in the **Nominative case.**

	M	F	N	PL
NOMINATIVE	ein	eine	ein	–
	der	die	das	die

e.g.	**ein**	Hund (*a dog*)		**der**	Hund (*the dog*)
	eine	Katze (*a cat*)		**die**	Katze (*the cat*)
	ein	Pferd (*a horse*)		**das**	Pferd (*the horse*)
		Tiere (*animals – no article before it*)		**die**	Tiere (*the animals*)

The Nominative case is used for the **subject** of the sentence.

14c The Accusative case

In the **Accusative case** articles change as follows:

	M	F	N	PL
ACCUSATIVE	**einen**	eine	ein	–
	den	die	das	die

As you can see, the **only difference** between the Nominative and Accusative is that **ein (M)** changes to **einen** and that **der** changes to **den**.

The Accusative case is used for the **direct object** of the sentence.

Look at this rhyme – it might be useful to learn it off by heart to help you remember the Accusative case.

NOMINATIVE	VERB	ACCUSATIVE	
Frau Bamster	hat	**einen** Hamster.	**M**
Klaus	hat	**eine** Maus.	**F**
Gerd	hat	**ein** Pferd.	**N**
Sabinchen	hat	zwölf Kaninchen	**PL**

Ich suche **den** Bahnhof.	*I'm looking for the station.*
Er sucht **die** Post.	*He is looking for the post office.*
Wir suchen **das** Jugendzentrum.	*We are looking for the youth centre.*
Haben Sie **einen** Stadtplan?	*Do you have a town map?*
Wir haben **eine** Broschüre und **ein** Poster.	*We have a brochure and a poster.*

14d Es gibt

This phrase is followed by the Accusative case and means 'there is/there are …'

Es gibt einen Sportplatz und eine Disko, aber **es gibt** kein Jugendzentrum.	*There is a sports ground and a disco, but not a youth centre.*
Gibt es eine Stadthalle?	*Is there a concert hall?*
Es gibt nicht genug Jobs.	*There aren't enough jobs.*

14e The Dative case

In the **Dative case** articles change even more, as follows:

	M	F	N	PL
DATIVE	**einem**	**einer**	**einem**	–
	dem	**der**	**dem**	**den**

Note: all nouns in the Dative plural add an **-n** whenever possible:

(die Berge)	in den Berge**n**	*in the mountains*
(die Häuser)	in den Häuser**n**	*in the houses*
(die Freunde)	bei Freunde**n**	*(staying) with friends*

but

(die Hotels)	in den Hotels	*in the hotels*

Prepositions

15a   Prepositions

Prepositions are words like 'in', 'on', 'under', 'through', 'by', 'for', etc.
In German all prepositions must be followed by particular cases.

15b   Some prepositions which are sometimes followed by the Accusative case, and sometimes by the Dative case

Here are some prepositions which are followed by either the Accusative, or the Dative case,
depending on whether movement is involved:

an	*to; by; on*	auf	*onto; on*	hinter	*behind*	in	*into; in*	vor	*in front of*

The **Accusative case** is used after these prepositions
when there is **movement to or away from** the place mentioned:

Wir fahren **an die** See.	*We're going to the seaside.*
Er geht **auf den** Balkon.	*He's going onto the balcony.*
Ralf der Räuber geht **in die** Bank.	*Ralf the Robber goes into the bank.*
Gehst du **ins** Schuhgeschäft?	*Are you going to the shoe shop?*

The **Dative case** is used after these prepositions
when there is **no movement to or away from** the place mentioned:

Das Ferienhaus ist **am** Meer.	*The holiday home is by the sea.*
Das ist **auf der** linken Seite.	*It's on the left hand side.*
Das Parkplatz ist **in der** Wittekindstraße.	*The car park is in Wittekindstraße.*
Das Auto ist **im** Parkhaus.	*The car is in the multistorey carpark.*
Das Verkehrsamt ist **hinter der** Kirche.	*The tourist office is behind the church.*
Die Bushaltestelle ist **vor dem** Dom.	*The bus stop is in front of the cathedral.*

Note also:

15c   Some prepositions which are always followed by the Accusative

Here are some prepositions which must always be followed by the **Accusative case**:

durch *through*	für	*for*	um	*round*

Ich fahre **durch die** Stadt.	*I drive through the town.*
Das ist **für meinen** Bruder.	*That's for my brother.*
Sie geht **um die** Ecke.	*She goes round the corner.*

15d   Some prepositions which are always followed by the Dative

Here are some prepositions which must always be followed by the **Dative case**:

aus	*out of; from*	mit	*with*	von	*from; of*
bei	*at (the home of)*	nach	*after*	zu	*to*

Er kommt **aus der** Schweiz.	*He comes from Switzerland.*
Bei mir zu Hause.	*At my house.*
Ich fahre **mit dem** Bus.	*I go by bus.*
Fährst du **mit der** Fähre nach England?	*Are you going to England by ferry?*
Nach dem Mittagessen spiele ich Tennis.	*After lunch I'm going to play tennis.*
Von welchem Gleis?	*From which platform?*
Wie kommst du **zum** Sportplatz?	*How are you getting to the sports ground?*
Wie komme ich **am** besten **zur** Stadthalle?	*What is the best way to the concert hall?*

15e   Contracted prepositions

Sometimes the preposition and article are combined:

am an dem	**im** in dem	**zum** zu dem	**beim** bei dem
ans an das	**ins** in das	**zur** zu der	

15f   Countries

Use **nach** when talking about going to most countries (+ towns and villages):

Ich fahre	**nach**	Italien/Spanien/Polen/Frankreich/Schottland/Nordirland. Berlin/München/Wien.
I'm going	to	Italy/Spain/Poland/France/Scotland/Northern Ireland. Berlin/Munich/Vienna.

But use **in die** with this country:

Ich fahre	**in die**	Schweiz.
I'm going	to	Switzerland.

Pronouns

16a   Pronouns

These are words like 'she', 'they', 'him', 'it' in English, which can replace nouns.

16b   Nominative case pronouns

ich	I	Ich spiele gern Fußball.	I like playing football
du	you	Wie alt bist du?	How old are you?
er	he	Er (= der Hund) heißt Rowdy.	He (the dog) is called Rowdy.
sie	she	Er (= der Wagen) ist rot.	It* (the car) is red.
es	it	Sie (= die Katze) heißt Mitzi.	She (the cat) is called Mitzi.
wir	we	Es (= das Pferd) heißt Rex.	He* (the horse) is called Rex.
ihr	you	Wir gehen in die Stadt.	We are going to town.
Sie	you (polite)	Habt ihr Geld dabei?	Have you got any money with you?
sie	they	Wie heißen Sie?	What are you called?
		Sie trinken gern Cola.	They like drinking coke.

***es** in German can sometimes be 'he' or 'she' in English, just as **er** and **sie** can mean 'it'.

16c   Accusative case pronouns

ich	**mich**	me	Der Dom interessiert **mich** nicht.	I'm not interested in the cathedral.
du	**dich**	you		
er	**ihn**	him	Wie findest du **ihn**?	What do you think of him?
sie	**sie**	her	Ich finde **sie** nett.	I think she's nice.
es	**es**	it		
wir	**uns**	us		
ihr	**euch**	you		
Sie	**Sie**	you (polite)	Das ist für **Sie**, Frau Schmidt.	That's for **you**, Mrs Schmidt.
sie	**sie**	them	Was kaufst du für **sie**?	What are you buying for them?

16d   Dative case pronouns

ich	**mir**	me, to me	**Mir** ist schlecht.	I don't feel well.
du	**dir**	you, to you	Was fehlt **dir**?	What's wrong (with **you**)?
er	**ihm**	him, to him	Es geht **ihm** gut.	He is fine.
sie	**ihr**	her, to her	Wie geht's **ihr**?	How is she?
es	**ihm**	it, to it		
wir	**uns**	us, to us	**Uns** ist zu warm.	We are too warm.
ihr	**euch**	you, to you		
Sie	**Ihnen**	you, to you	Kann ich **Ihnen** helfen?	Can I help **you**?
sie	**ihnen**	them, to them		

16e   Some special verbs requiring Dative pronouns

gefallen

Gefällt **dir** die Kassette?	Do you like the cassette?
Gefallen **deiner Mutter** die Handschuhe?	Does your mother like the gloves?
Die Bluse gefällt **mir**.	I like the blouse.
Wie gefällt **ihnen** das Geschenk?	How do they like the present?

schmecken

Wie schmeckt **dir** der Kuchen?	Do you like the cake?
Schmeckt es **dir**?	Do you like it?

gehen *(meaning how someone is)*

Es geht **mir** gut, danke.	I'm fine, thank you.

Adjectives

17a   Adjectives

Adjectives are words which describe nouns. They have no endings in sentences like this:

Jürgen ist **toll**.	*Jürgen is great.*	Annette ist **nett**.	*Annette is nice.*	Das ist **billig**.	*That's cheap.*

More information can be given to an adjective by using a 'qualifier' or an 'intensifier':

Die Stadt ist **ganz** schön.	The town is really nice.
Das Meer ist **sehr** schmutzig.	The sea is very dirty.
Er ist **nicht sehr** sympathisch.	He's not very nice.
Die Schule ist **ziemlich** klein.	The school is quite small.
Sie ist **unheimlich** nett.	She is ever so nice.

17b   Too much/too many

Es gibt **zu viel** Rauch. Es gibt **zu viele** Touristen.	There is too much smoke. There are too many tourists.

17c   Adjectival agreement

When adjectives are used next to a noun they have different endings. These depend on the gender and case of the noun, whether it is singular or plural and any other word which is used before it. This is called adjectival agreement.

	M	F	N	PL
NOMINATIVE	ein alter Mann	eine alte Frau	ein altes Pferd	alte Bücher
ACCUSATIVE	einen alten Mann	eine alte Frau	ein altes Pferd	alte Bücher
DATIVE	einem alten Mann	einer alten Frau	einem alten Pferd	alten Büchern

	M	F	N	PL
NOMINATIVE	der alte Mann	die alte Frau	das alte Pferd	die alten Bücher
ACCUSATIVE	den alten Mann	die alte Frau	das alte Pferd	die alten Bücher
DATIVE	dem alten Mann	der alten Frau	dem alten Pferd	den alten Büchern

Die **grüne** Hose gefällt mir.	I like the green trousers.
Er trägt einen **blauen** Pullover und ein **schwarzes** T-Shirt.	He is wearing a blue pullover and a black t-shirt.
Sie hat **glatte**, **blonde** Haare und **blaue** Augen.	She has straight, blond hair and blue eyes.

17d   Mein, dein, sein (possessive adjectives) and kein

Mein, **dein**, **sein** and **kein** *follow this pattern:*

	M	F	N	PL
NOMINATIVE	mein	meine	mein	meine
ACCUSATIVE	meinen	meine	mein	meine
DATIVE	meinem	meiner	meinem	meinen

In the singular, the pattern is the same as **ein**, **eine**, **ein**.

Dies ist **mein** Vater.	*This is my father.*	Ist das **deine** Mutter?	*Is that your mother?*
Er hat **keinen** Hund.	*He doesn't have a dog.*	Hast du **keine** Katze?	*Haven't you got a cat?*
Du hast **mein** Heft!	*You've got my book!*	**Sein** Pullover ist gelb.	*His pullover is yellow.*
Das ist in **meinem** Heft.	*That is in my exercise book.*	**Ihre** Augen sind blau.	*Her eyes are blue.*

Ihr *(her),* **euer** *(your) and* **unser** *(our) also follow the same pattern.*

17e Comparitives and superlatives

To say 'cheaper', 'more expensive', 'nicer' etc. (comparitives) add **-er** *to the adjective:*

In Helgoland ist Fleisch **billiger** als in Deutschland.	Meat is cheaper in Helgoland than in Germany.
Dieser Campingplatz ist **kleiner**.	This campsite is smaller.

But note that **besser** *means 'better'.*

Note also that **am besten** *means 'the best' (superlative):*

Am besten fliegen wir.	The best thing to do is to fly.

17f Too ...

To say 'too expensive', 'too far', etc. use **zu** *with an adjective:*

Das ist **zu teuer**.	That's too expensive.
Italien ist **zu weit** weg.	Italy is too far away.
In England ist es **zu kalt**.	It's too cold in England.

Word order

18a Word order

There are various rules in German governing where words should be placed in a sentence.

18b Main clauses

Most of the sentences in this book are called **main clauses**.
Except when asking questions like **Hast du ...?**, **Kommst du ...?** *(see section 4),*
the verb is always the **second** *piece of information:*

1	2 (VERB)	3	
Ich	heiße	Peter.	I'm called Peter.
Mein Name	ist	Krull.	My name is Krull.
Wie	heißt	du?	What are you called?

Because the verb must be the second piece of information, this sometimes means that the order of the parts in the sentence is different from the English:

Heute Abend gebe ich eine Party.	I'm having a party this evening.
Morgen gehe ich ins Kino.	I'm going to the cinema tomorrow.
Um wie viel Uhr isst du dein Mittagessen?	When do you eat lunch?
Dann gehe ich zur Schule.	Then I go to school.
Einige Minuten später kommt Anna ins Zimmer.	A few minutes later Anna comes into the room.

18c Sentences with more than one verb

When there are two verbs in a sentence, the second verb is usually in the **infinitive**.
(See sections **11n**, **11o** *and* **11p**.*)*

The infinitive is **at the end of the sentence:**

	FIRST VERB		INFINITIVE	
Ich	gehe	gern	**schwimmen**.	I like going swimming.
Wo	kann	ich Postkarten	**kaufen**?	Where can I buy postcards?
Du	kannst	zu uns	**kommen**.	You can come to our house.
Was	willst	du	**sehen**?	What do you want to see?

18d   When? How? Where? in the same sentence.

In a German sentence, if two or more of these elements are present, they should come in this order:

1 When? (Time)	2 How? (Manner)	3 Where? (Place)

*If a time and a place are mentioned, the **time** comes before the **place**:*

TIME		PLACE
Nächste Woche	fahre ich	**nach München.**

Next week I'm going to Munich.

or

	TIME	PLACE
Ich fahre	**nächste Woche**	**nach München.**

Next week I'm going to Munich.

*If you say **how** you are going somewhere, this must come **before** the **place**:*

	MANNER	PLACE
Ich fahre	**mit dem Bus**	**zum Schwimmbad.**

I'm going to the swimming pool by bus.

*If you say **when, how** and **where** you are going, they must go in that order:*

	TIME	MANNER	PLACE
Ich fahre	**nächste Woche**	**mit dem Zug**	**nach Köln.**

Next week, I'm going to Cologne by train.

Likes and favourites

19a   Talking about what you like doing

Gern *can be used with most verbs to show that you **like** doing something:*

Ich trinke Kaffee.	*I drink coffee.*
Ich trinke **gern** Kaffee.	*I **like** drinking coffee.*
Ich gehe schwimmen.	*I go swimming.*
Ich gehe **gern** schwimmen.	*I **like** going swimming.*

*Notice how you say that you like **something** (a noun):*

Ich **habe** Katzen **gern.**	*I **like** cats.*
Ich **mag** Tee**.**	*I **like** tea.*

19b   Talking about what you prefer doing

Lieber *can be used with most verbs to show that you **prefer** doing something:*

Ich fliege **lieber**.	*I **prefer** flying.*
Ich fahre **lieber** mit dem Zug.	*I **prefer** travelling by train.*

19c   Talking about what you like doing most of all

*Start the sentence with **am liebsten**, and remember that the next thing must be a verb:*

Am liebsten spiele ich Fußball.	*I **like** playing football **most of all**.*
Am liebsten gehe ich schwimmen.	*I **like** going swimming **most of all**.*

*Note also the use of **Lieblings-** with a noun:*

Fußball ist mein **Lieblingssport.**	*Football is my **favourite** sport.*
Mein **Lieblingsfach** ist Deutsch.	*My **favourite** lesson is German.*

A

	ab from
der	**Abend(e)** evening
	abends in the evening
das	**Abendkleid(er)** evening dress
	aber but
die	**Abfahrt(en)** departure
der	**Abflug(¨e)** take-off, flight
	ab/schicken to send off
	absolut absolute(ly)
	ach oh dear
	acht eight
	achtzehn eighteen
	achtzig eighty
die	**Adjektive(n)** adjective
der	**Admiral(e)** admiral
die	**Adresse(n)** address
	ähnlich similar
die	**Ahnung(en)** idea, notion
	keine Ahnung! haven't a clue!
	alkoholisch alcoholic
	alle(s) all, everything
	allein alone
die	**Allergie(n)** allergy
	allergisch (gegen) allergic to
	als as; than; when
	also so, therefore
	alt old
das	**Alter** age
die	**Altstadt(¨e)** old part of town
	Amerika America
	an (+ Acc/Dat) to, at, on
das	**Andenken(-)** souvenir
	ander(er/e/es) other
	anderthalb one and a half
	an/fordern to request
	angekommen arrived (from **ankommen**)
das	**Angeln** fishing
	angeln to fish
die	**Ankunft(¨e)** arrival
die	**Anmeldung(en)** registration
die	**Annonce(n)** advertisement
der	**Anorak(s)** anorak
	an/rufen to telephone
	anschließend then, after that
	an/sehen to look at
die	**Antwort(en)** answer
	antworten to answer
der	**Anzug(¨e)** suit
der	**Apfel(¨)** apple
der	**Apfelsaft** apple juice
die	**Apotheke(n)** chemist's shop
der	**April** April
die	**Arbeit(en)** work, job
	arbeiten to work
der	**Arm(e)** arm

die	**Armbanduhr(en)** wrist watch
	arm poor
der	**Artikel(-)** article
die	**Aspirintablette(n)** aspirin
	Aua! ouch!
	auch also, too
	auf (+ Acc/Dat) on, onto
	aufgrund because of
	auf/schreiben to write down
das	**Auge(n)** eye
der	**August** August
	aus (+ Dat) out of
	auseinander apart
die	**Ausfahrt(en)** exit (motorway)
der	**Ausflug(¨e)** excursion
der	**Ausgang(¨e)** exit
	aus/geben to spend (money)
	aus/gehen to go out
die	**Auskunft(¨e)** information
die	**Ausrede(n)** excuse
	aus/sehen to look, appear
das	**Aussehen** appearance
	außerdem besides
	außerhalb outside
der	**Aussichtsturm(¨e)** observation tower
	Australien Australia
das	**Auto(s)** car
die	**Autobahn(en)** motorway
	autofrei no cars allowed
der	**Autowaschplatz(¨e)** car wash

B

das	**Babysitten** babysitting
der	**Babysitter(-)** babysitter
die	**Bäckerei(en)** bakery, breadshop
die	**Backwaren** (pl) cookies, biscuits
die	**Badehose(n)** bathing trunks
die	**Bademütze(n)** bathing cap
der	**Badesee(n)** lake for bathing
das	**Badetuch(¨er)** bath towel
der	**Badmintonschläger(-)** badminton raquet
die	**Bahn(en)** train
	mit der Bahn by train
der	**Bahnhof(¨e)** station
das	**Bahnhofsrestaurant(s)** station restaurant
der	**Bahnsteig(e)** platform
	bald soon
die	**Banane(n)** banana
die	**Bank(en)** bank
die	**Bar(s)** bar, night-club
	bar cash
	beantworten to answer
der	**Becher(-)** tub
sich	**befinden** to be situated

der	**Beginn** beginning
	beginnen to begin
	begründen to give reasons for
	beheizt heated
	bei (+ Dat) by; with; at the house of
	beides both
	bei/legen to enclose
das	**Bein(e)** leg
das	**Beispiel(e)** example
	zum Beispiel for example
	bekommen to get, receive
	belegt covered
	belegtes Brot sandwich
der	**Benzinverbrauch** petrol consumption
	bequem comfortable
der	**Berg(e)** mountain
	beschreiben to describe
	beschriften to label
	besichtigen to inspect, view
etwas	**Besonderes** something special
nichts	**Besonderes** nothing special
	besser better
die	**Besserung** recovery
	gute Besserung get well soon
	best(er/e/es) best
	bestehen aus to consist of
	bestimmt definitely
der	**Besuch(e)** visit
	besuchen to visit
das	**Bett(en)** bed
die	**Bettwäsche** bed linen
der	**BH** bra
die	**Bibliothek(en)** library
das	**Bier(e)** beer
die	**Bierwurst(¨e)** beer sausage
der	**Bikini(s)** bikini
das	**Bild(er)** picture
	bilden to form, build
die	**Bildgeschichte(n)** picture story
die	**Bildvokabeln** (pl) picture vocabulary
	billig cheap
ich	**bin** I am (from **sein**)
	bis until
ein	**bisschen** a bit, a little
du	**bist** you are (from **sein**)
	bitte please
	bitten to ask
	blau blue
	bleiben to stay
der	**Bleistift(e)** pencil
der	**Blitz** lightning
	blöd stupid
	blond blonde
	bloß just
die	**Blume(n)** flower

der	**Blumenstrauß(ˇe)** bunch of flowers	
der	**Blumentopf(ˇe)** flower pot	
die	**Bluse(n)** blouse	
der	**Bootsverleih** boat hire	
der	**Brand(ˇe)** fire	
die	**Brandwunde(n)** burn injury	
	brauchen to need	
	braun brown	
der	**Brief(e)** letter	
der	**Briefkasten(ˇ)** letter-box	
die	**Briefmarke(n)** stamp	
die	**Brille(n)** pair of glasses	
	bringen to bring	
die	**Brise(n)** breeze	
	britisch British	
die	**Broschüre(n)** brochure, leaflet	
das	**Brot(e)** bread, loaf	
das	**Brötchen(-)** roll	
der	**Bruder(ˇ)** brother	
das	**Buch(ˇer)** book	
die	**Buchhandlung(en)** book shop	
die	**Buchung(en)** reservation	
das	**Bügeleisen(-)** iron	
die	**Bundesliga** federal football league	
	bunt coloured, colourful	
das	**Büro(s)** office	
der	**Bus(se)** bus	
der	**Busbahnhof(ˇe)** bus station	
der	**Busfahrplan(ˇe)** bus timetable	
die	**Bushaltestelle(n)** bus stop	
die	**Buslinie(n)** bus route	
die	**Butter** butter	

C

das	**Café(s)** café
der	**Camping** camping
der	**Campingbus(se)** camper van
der	**Campingplatz(ˇe)** campsite
die	**Campingplatzregel(n)** campsite rule
die	**CD(s)** compact disc
der	**CD-Spieler(-)** CD-player
die	**Clique(n)** group, set
die	**Cola(s)** coke
der	**Computer(-)** computer
der	**Computerklub(s)** computer club
das	**Computerspiel(e)** computer game
der	**Cousin(s)** cousin (male)

D

	da there	
	dabei present, there	
	dagegen against it	
	dahin there (with verb of movement)	
die	**Dame(n)** lady	
die	**Damenmode(n)** ladies' fashion	
die	**Damentoilette(n)** ladies' toilet	
	danach after that	
	danke thank you	
	vielen Dank many thanks	
	danken to thank	
	dann then	
ich	**darf** I may (from **dürfen**)	
du	**darfst** you may (from **dürfen**)	
	darüber about it, over it	
	das the (n); this, that	
	dass that	
	dauern to last	
	davon from it; of it	
	dazu to it; in addition	
	dein(e) your	
	denken to think	
	denn for, because	
	der/die/das the; who (m/f/n)	
der	**Deutschlehrer(-)** German teacher	
	Deutschland Germany	
der	**Dezember** December	
das	**Diagramm(e)** diagram	
der	**Dialog(e)** dialogue	
	dich you (Acc)	
	dick fat, thick	
	die the (f/pl)	
der	**Dienstag** Tuesday	
	dies(er/e/es) this, these	
	diktieren to dictate	
	dir to you (Dat)	
	direkt direct, straight	
die	**Disko(s)** disco	
der	**Diskofan(s)** disco fan	
die	**DM (Deutschmark)** German mark	
	doch however, but, yet	
der	**Doktor(en)** doctor	
der	**Dom(e)** cathedral	
der	**Donnerstag** Thursday	
	doof stupid	
das	**Dorf(ˇer)** village	
	dort there	
	dorthin there (with verb of movement)	
die	**Dose(n)** tin, can	
	dran/sein to have one's turn	
	ich bin dran it's my turn	
	drei three	

	dreihundert three hundred	
	dreimal three times	
	dreizehn thirteen	
	dritt(er/e/es) third	
die	**Drogerie(n)** chemist's	
	drüben over there	
der	**Drucker(-)** printer	
	du you (informal)	
die	**Düne(n)** dune	
	dunkel dark	
	durch through	
das	**Durcheinander** muddle	
	durcheinander in a muddle	
die	**Dusche(n)** shower	

E

	egal equal	
	es ist mir egal it's all the same to me, I'm not bothered	
	ehrlich honest	
das	**Eichhörnchen(-)** squirrel	
	eigen(er/e/es) own	
	eigentlich actually, really	
	ein(e) a; one	
	einfach easy; single (ticket)	
die	**Einfahrt(en)** access road (motorway)	
der	**Eingang(ˇe)** entrance	
die	**Einheit(en)** unit	
	einige some	
der	**Einkauf(ˇe)** purchase	
	Ich mache Einkäufe I do some shopping	
	ein/kaufen to shop	
das	**Einkaufslied(er)** shopping song	
die	**Einkaufsliste(n)** shopping list	
die	**Einladung(en)** invitation	
	einmal once	
die	**Einrichtungen** (pl) furnishings	
	eins one	
der	**Eintritt(e)** entrance, admission charge	
das	**Eis** ice cream	
die	**Eisdiele(n)** ice cream parlour	
	elf eleven	
die	**Eltern** (pl) parents	
	empfehlen to recommend	
das	**Ende(n)** end	
	England England	
der	**Engländer(-)** Englishman	
die	**Engländerin(nen)** Englishwoman	
	Englisch English (lang)	
	englisch (adj) English	
	entfernt distant	
	entschuldigen to excuse	
	Entschuldigung! Sorry!	

der **Entschuldigungszettel(-)** absence note

entweder ... oder ... either ... or ...

er he; it

das **Erdgeschoss** ground floor

erfinden to invent

die **Erkältung(en)** cold, chill

die **Ermäßigung(en)** reduction, discount

erraten to guess

erreichen to reach

ersetzen to replace

erst only; not until

erst(er/e/es) first

der **Erwachsene(n)** adult

es it

das **Essen** food, meal

essen to eat

etwa approximately

etwas something

euch you (informal pl)

die **Eule(n)** owl

die **Europa-Tournee(n)** European tour

F

die **Fabrik(en)** factory

die **Fähre(n)** ferry

mlt der Fähre by ferry

fahren to travel, drive

die **Fahrkarte(n)** ticket

der **Fahrkartenautomat(en)** ticket machine

der **Fahrplan("e)** timetable

das **Fahrrad("er)** bicycle

der **Fahrradweg(e)** cycle path

die **Fahrt(en)** journey

fair fair

falsch wrong

die **Familie(n)** family

der **Familienbesuch** family visit

das **Familienmitglied(er)** member of family

fantastisch fantastic

die **Farbe(n)** colour

fast almost

der **Februar** February

Federball badminton

fehlen to be missing

was fehlt dir? what's wrong with you?

fein fine, splendid

die **Feinkost** delicatessen

das **Feld(er)** field

der **Felsen(-)** rock

das **Fenster(-)** window

die **Ferien** (pl) holidays

fern far, distant

ferngesehen watched television (from **fernsehen**)

das **Fernsehen** television

fern/sehen to watch television

der **Fernseher(-)** television set

die **Fernsehzeitung(en)** TV guide

fertig ready, finished

das **Fertiggericht(e)** ready-made meal

das **Fieber** fever, high temperature

fies horrible

der **Film(e)** film

finden to find

der **Fisch(e)** fish

fit fit

die **Flasche(n)** bottle

das **Fleisch** meat

fleißig hard working

fliegen to fly

die **Flöte(n)** flute

der **Flug("e)** flight

die **Flugangst** fear of flying

der **Flughafen(")** airport

der **Flugplan("e)** flight timetable

der **Flugplatz("e)** airport

der **Flugpreis(e)** price of flight

das **Flugzeug(e)** aeroplane

der **Fluss(Flüsse)** river

folgend following

das **Formular(e)** form

das **Foto(s)** photo

das **Fotoalbum(-alben)** photograph album

der **Fotoapparat(e)** camera

fotografieren to take photographs

die **Frage(n)** question

fragen to ask

Frankreich France

die **Frau(en)** woman, Mrs.

frei free, vacant

das **Freibad("er)** open-air pool

der **Freitag** Friday

fremd strange, foreign

der **Freund(e)** friend (male)

die **Freundin(nen)** friend (female)

freundlich friendly, kind

früh early

das **Frühstück** breakfast

fühlen to feel

das **Fundbüro(s)** lost property office

fünf five

fünfhundert five hundred

fünft(er/e/es) fifth

fünfzehn fifteen

fünfzig fifty

für for

fürchterlich terrible

der **Fuß("e)** foot

zu Fuß on foot

der **Fußball(bälle)** football

der **Fußballschuh(e)** football boot

das **Fußballspiel(e)** football match

das **Fußballstadion(-stadien)** football stadium

die **Fußgängerzone(n)** pedestrian precinct

G

ganz quite; whole

gar nicht not at all

der **Garten(")** garden

der **Gast("e)** guest

das **Gasthaus("er)** hotel, restaurant

gearbeitet worked (from **arbeiten**)

geben to give

er gibt he gives

das **Gebiet(e)** area, district

geblieben stayed (from **bleiben**)

gebrochen broken (from **brechen**)

der **Geburtstag(e)** birthday

die **Geburtstagsfeier(n)** birthday party

die **Geburtstagskarte(n)** birthday card

das **Gedicht(e)** poem

geehrt(e/r) Dear (in formal letters)

geeignet suitable

gefahren travelled, driven (from **fahren**)

gefallen to please

es gefällt mir I like it

gefallen fallen (from **fallen**)

das **Gefängnis(se)** prison

gefeiert celebrated (from **feiern**)

geflogen flown (from **fliegen**)

gegangen gone (from **gehen**)

gegeben given (from **geben**)

gegen against

die **Gegend** area, district

gegessen eaten (from **essen**)

gehen to go

das geht (nicht) that's OK (that won't do)

wie geht's? how are you?

gehört heard (from **hören**)

gekauft bought (from **kaufen**)

gekommen come (from **kommen**)

gelb yellow

das **Geld** money

der **Geldwechsel** money exchange

gemacht made, done (from **machen**)

das **Gemüse** vegetables

genau exact(ly)

das **Genie(s)** genius

genug enough

genügend sufficient

die **Gepäckaufbewahrung** left luggage office

gerade straight, just

geradeaus straight ahead

gern(e) gladly
ich esse gern Eis I like ice cream

die **Gesamtschule(n)** comprehensive school

die **Gesamtsumme(n)** total amount

das **Geschäft(e)** shop

der **Geschäftsname(n)** name of shop

das **Geschenk(e)** present

die **Geschichte(n)** story, history

geschlafen slept (from **schlafen**)

geschlossen closed (from **schließen**)

geschmeckt tasted (from **schmecken**)

geschrieben written (from **schreiben**)

die **Geschwister** (pl) brothers and sisters

gesehen seen (from **sehen**)

das **Gesicht(er)** face

das **Gespräch(e)** conversation

gesprochen spoken (from **sprechen**)

gestattet allowed

gestern yesterday

gestreift striped

gesucht looked for (from **suchen**)

gesund healthy, well

getanzt danced (from **tanzen**)

getragen worn; carried (from **tragen**)

das **Getränk(e)** drink

getroffen met (from **treffen**)

getrunken drunk (from **trinken**)

gewesen been (from **sein**)

er/sie/es **gibt** he/she/it gives (from **geben**)

es **gibt** there is/there are

er/sie/es **ging** he/she/it went (from **gehen**)

das **Girl(s)** girl

die **Gitarre(n)** guitar

das **Glas(¨er)** glass; jar

glatt smooth; straight (hair)

glauben to believe

gleich the same; at once

das **Gleis(e)** platform

das **Glück** luck

die **Glückseligkeit** happiness

der **Goldfisch(e)** goldfish

der **Graf(en)** count

die **Graffiti** graffiti

die **Graffitimauer(n)** graffiti wall

das **Gramm** gramme

grau grey

die **Grenze(n)** border, frontier

die **Grillhütte(n)** barbecue hut

die **Grillparty** barbecue

die **Grippe** flu

groß big

die **Größe(n)** size

die **Großmutter(¨)** grandmother

der **Großvater(¨)** grandfather

grün green

die **Grundschule(n)** primary school

die **Gruppe(n)** group

die **Gruppenarbeit** group work

das **Gruppenfoto(s)** group photo

grüß dich! hello there!

der **Gruß(¨e)** greeting
mit herzlichen Grüßen with best wishes (in letters)

gucken to look

die **Gummibärchen** (pl) jelly bears

der **Gummistiefel(-)** Wellington boot

gut good
alles Gute all the best

H

das **Haar(e)** hair

haarig hairy

haben to have

haften (für) to take responsibility for

halb half

das **Hallenbad(¨er)** indoor swimming pool

hallo! hello!

die **Halskette(n)** necklace

die **Halsschmerzen** (pl) sore throat

die **Haltestelle(n)** bus stop

der **Hamburger(-)** Hamburger

der **Hammer(¨)** hammer

die **Hand(¨e)** hand

das **Handgelenk(e)** wrist

der **Handschuh(e)** glove

hassen to hate

du **hast** you have (from **haben**)

er/sie/es **hat** he/she/it has (from **haben**)

ich **hatte** I had (from **haben**)

der **Hauptbahnhof(¨e)** main station

die **Hauptreisezeit** peak travel time

die **Hauptsaison(s)** high season

die **Hauptstadt(¨e)** capital city

das **Haus(¨er)** house
nach Hause (to) home
zu Hause at home

die **Hausaufgaben** (pl) homework

die **Haustiernahrung** pet food

das **Heft(e)** exercise book

die **Heilkraft** healing power

heißen to be called

helfen to help
er hilft he helps

hellbraun light brown

das **Hemd(en)** shirt

der **Herr(en)** gentleman, Mr

die **Herrenmode(n)** men's fashion

die **Herrentoilette(n)** men's toilet

der **Heuschnupfen** hay fever

heute today

hier here

die **Hilfe** help

er/sie/es **hilft** he/she/it helps (from **helfen**)

hin und her to and fro
hin und zurück return ticket

hinten at the back

hinter (+ Acc/Dat) behind

die **Hirnmasse** brain

die **Hitparade** hit parade

das **Hobby(s)** hobby

hoch high

hoffentlich it is to be hoped

holen to fetch

der **Honig** honey

hören to hear

das **Höschen** girl's pants

die **Hose(n)** trousers

das **Hotel(s)** hotel

die **Hotelliste(n)** list of hotels

der **Hund(e)** dog

hundert hundred

der **Hustenbonbon(s)** cough sweet

das **Hypochonderlied(er)** hypochondriac's song

I

der **IC-Zug(¨e)** Intercity train

ich I

ideal ideal

die **Idee(n)** idea

ihm (Dat) to him

ihn (Acc) him

ihnen (Dat pl) to them

Ihnen (Dat) to you (formal)

ihr you (informal pl); to her (Dat)
ihr(e) her; their
Ihr(e) your (formal)
das Image image
immer always
in (+ Acc/Dat) in, into
die Information(en) information
das Informationsmaterial informatory material
inkl.(= inklusiv) inclusive
die Insel(n) island
das Inselparadies island paradise
interessieren to interest
das ist that is
er/sie/es ist he/she/it/one is
Italien Italy

J

ja yes
die Jacke(n) jacket
das Jahr(e) year
der Januar January
je ever; per
je Person per person
die Jeans (pl) jeans
jed(er/e/es) each, every
jemand someone
jetzt now
der Job(s) job
der Jogurt(s) yoghurt
der Jugendklub(s) youth club
die Jugendherberge(n) youth hostel
der/die Jugendliche(n) young person
der Jugendraum(¨e) room for young people
das Jugendzentrum(-zentren) youth centre
der Juli July
jung young
der Junge(n) boy
der Juni June

K

der Kaffee coffee
kalt cold
das Kamel(e) camel
der Kanal(¨e) canal
das Kaninchen(-) rabbit
ich kann I can (from können)
du kannst you can (from können)
die Kapsel(n) capsule
die Karotte(n) carrot
die Karte(n) card
die Kartoffel(n) potato

der Käse cheese
die Kasse(n) till; ticket office
die Kassette(n) cassette
das Kästchen(-) small box
der Kasten(¨) box
kaufen to buy
das Kaufhaus(¨er) department store
die Kegelbahn(en) bowling alley
das Kegeln bowling
kein(e) no, not any
der Keks(e) biscuit
kennen gelernt got to know (from kennen lernen)
kennen to know (a person)
der Kerl(e) fellow, chap
das Kettenspiel(e) chain game
das Kilo(s) kilogramme
der Kilometer(-) kilometre
das Kind(er) child
die Kindermode(n) children's fashion
das Kinderschwimmbecken(-) children's pool
der Kinderspielplatz(¨e) children's playground
das Kino(s) cinema
der Kiosk(e) kiosk
die Kirche(n) church
die Klamotten (pl) (slang) clothes
klar clear
die Klasse(n) class
erste/zweite Klasse first/second class
die Klassenarbeit(en) classwork
die Klassenfahrt(en) class trip
der/die Klassenlehrer/in class teacher
das Kleid(er) dress
die Kleider (pl) clothes
das Kleidergeschäft(¨e) clothes shop
der Kleiderschrank(¨e) wardrobe
das Kleidungsstück(e) item of clothing
klein small
kochen to cook
der Kofferkuli(s) luggage trolley
kommen to come
kompliziert complicated
die Konditorei(en) cake shop
die Konfirmation(en) confirmation
die Konfitüre(n) jam
können to be able
ich konnte I could, was able (from können)
die Konserven (pl) tinned food
das Konzert(e) concert
der Kopf(¨e) head
der Kopfhörer(-) headphone
das Kopfkissen(-) pillow

die Kopfschmerzen (pl) headache
die Kosmetik cosmetics
kostenlos free
kosten to cost
krank ill
das Krankenhaus(¨er) hospital
der Krankenhausaufenthalt stay in hospital
die Krankheit(en) illness
der Kuchen(-) cake
die Kurverwaltung spa administration
kurz short
in Kürze in brief
die Kusine(n) cousin (female)

L

lachen to laugh
die Lampe(n) lamp
das Land(¨er) country
das Landbrot(e) farm loaf
die Landkarte(n) map
lang long
lange for a long time
langweilig boring
laufen to run
laut loud
das Leben(-) life
die Lebensmittel (pl) food, groceries
die Leberwurst liver sausage
die Lederjacke(n) leather jacket
leer empty
leeren to empty
die Leerung(en) collection (of post)
legen to put
der Lehrer(-) teacher
die Lehrerin(nen) teacher
leiden to suffer
ich kann ihn nicht leiden I can't bear him
leider unfortunately
leise soft(ly)
lernen to learn
lesen to read
das Lesen reading
der Leser(-) reader
letzt(er/e/es) last
die Leute (pl) people
lieb dear, kind
Liebe/Lieber Dear (in letters)
lieber preferably
ich fliege lieber I prefer to fly
die Lieblings-CD(s) favourite CD
der/die Lieblingssänger(in) favourite singer

am	**liebsten** best of all
	liegen to lie
	lies! read! (from **lesen**)
er/sie/es	**liest** he/she/it reads (from **lesen**)
die	**Linie(n)** route (of bus); line
	link(er/e/es) left
	links on the left
die	**Liste(n)** list
der	**Liter(-)** litre
	lockig curly
	Los! Let's go!
was ist	**los?** what's the matter?
die	**Lücke(n)** gap
die	**Lust** wish, desire
	Hast du Lust …? Do you want to …?

M

	machen to do, make
	das macht that comes to
das	**Mädchen(-)** girl
ich	**mag** I like (from **mögen**)
die	**Magenschmerzen** (pl) stomachache
der	**Mai** May
das	**Make-up** make-up
das	**Mal** time
	Moment mal! just a moment!
	man one, they, people, you
	manchmal sometimes
der	**Mann(¨er)** man
die	**Margarine** margarine
die	**Mark** mark (money)
der	**Markt(¨e)** market
der	**Marktplatz(¨e)** market place
der	**Marsriegel(-)** Mars bar
der	**März** March
die	**Mathe** maths
die	**Mauer(n)** wall
die	**Maus(¨e)** mouse
das	**Medikament(e)** medicine, drug
das	**Meer(e)** sea
	mehr more
	mehrmals several times
	mein(e) my
	meinen to think
die	**Meinung(en)** opinion
der	**Meinungsmeter** opinion meter
die	**meisten** most
	meistens mostly
	melden to report
die	**Menge(n)** crowd, quantity
	jede Menge any amount
der	**Mensch(en)** person
	Mensch! Good heavens!
das	**Metal(e)** metal
das	**Meter(-)** metre

die	**Metzgerei(en)** butcher's shop
	mich (Acc) me
der	**Mikrofon** microphone
die	**Milch** milk
das	**Milchprodukt(e)** dairy product
der	**Milkshake** milkshake
der	**Minigolf** minigolf
der	**Minirock(¨e)** miniskirt
die	**Minute(n)** minute
	mir (Dat) to me
	mit (+ Dat) with
	mit/fahren to go with someone (vehicle)
	mit/kommen to come with someone
der	**Mitschüler(-)** fellow pupil (boy)
die	**Mitschülerin(nen)** fellow pupil (girl)
	mit/singen to join in singing
der	**Mittag** midday
	mittelgroß medium sized
	mittellang medium length
	mitten in (+ Dat) in the middle of
der	**Mittwoch** Wednesday
das	**Möbel** furniture
ich	**möchte** I should like (from **mögen**)
du	**möchtest** you would like (from **mögen**)
die	**Mode(n)** fashion
	modern modern
das	**Mofa(s)** moped
der	**Moment(e)** moment
	Moment mal! just a moment!
der	**Monat(e)** month
der	**Montag** Monday
der	**Morgen(-)** morning
	Guten Morgen! Good morning!
	morgen tomorrow
die	**Mücke(n)** gnat
	müde tired
die	**Muschel(n)** shellfish, mussel
das	**Museum(Museen)** museum
die	**Musik** music
ich	**muss** I must, have to (from **müssen**)
	müssen to have to
die	**Mutter(¨)** mother
	Mutti Mum

N

	na/na ja well
	nach after; to
der	**Nachmittag(e)** afternoon
die	**Nachsaison** late season
	nächst(er/e/es) next

die	**Nacht(¨e)** night
der	**Nachteil(e)** disadvantage
	nackt naked
in der	**Nähe** nearby
der	**Name(n)** name
	nämlich that is to say; you see
die	**Nasenspitze(n)** tip of the nose
	natürlich of course
	negativ negative
	nehmen to take
	nein no
	nee no (colloquial)
	nennen to call
	nett nice
	neu new
	neun nine
	nicht not
	nichts nothing
	nie never
	niemand nobody
	noch still
	noch nicht not yet
	nochmal once more
	Norddeutschland North Germany
im	**Norden** in the north
die	**Nordsee** North Sea
	normalerweise normally, usually
der	**Notausgang(¨e)** emergency exit
der	**November** November
die	**Nummer(n)** number
	nur only

O

	oben at the top; upstairs
das	**Obst** fruit
	oder or
	ohne (+ Acc) without
das	**Ohr(en)** ear
die	**Ohrenschmerzen** (pl) earache
der	**Ohrring(e)** ear ring
der	**Oktober** October
das	**Olympiastadion** Olympic stadium
das	**Olympiazentrum** Olympic centre
die	**Oma** grandma
der	**Onkel(-)** uncle
der	**Opa** grandpa
die	**Oper(n)** opera
das	**Orchester(-)** orchestra
im	**Osten** in the east
	Österreich Austria

P

das	**Paar(e)**	pair; couple
ein	**paar**	a few
die	**Packung(en)**	packet
das	**Parfüm**	perfume
der	**Park(s)**	park
das	**Parkhaus(¨er)**	multi-storey car park
der	**Parkplatz(¨e)**	car park, parking space
der	**Partner(-)**	partner (boy)
die	**Partnerarbeit**	pairwork
die	**Partnerin(nen)**	partner (girl)
die	**Party(s)**	party
	passend	suitable
	passen	to fit, to suit
das	**Pech**	bad luck
die	**Person(en)**	person
der	**Pfennig**	German coin (100Pf =1DM)
der	**Pfiff**	flair, style
die	**Pflanze(n)**	plant
das	**Pflaster(-)**	plaster
das	**Pfund(-)**	pound
der	**Pickel(-)**	spot, pimple
das	**Picknick**	picnic
die	**Pistole(n)**	pistol
die	**Pizza(s)**	pizza
der	**PKW(s)**	private car
der	**Plan(¨e)**	plan
	planen	to plan
der	**Platz(¨e)**	seat; square
	plötzlich	suddenly
der	**Polizist(en)**	policeman
das	**Polohemd(en)**	polo-necked shirt
die	**Popgruppe(n)**	pop group
das	**Popkonzert(e)**	pop concert
der	**Popstar(s)**	pop star
das	**Portmonee(s)**	purse
	positiv	positive
die	**Post**	post
das	**Poster(-)**	poster
die	**Postkarte(n)**	postcard
	praktisch	practical(ly)
die	**Praline(n)**	chocolate
der	**Preis(e)**	price
die	**Preisliste(n)**	price list
die	**Preissensation(en)**	sensational price
	preiswert	reasonable, worth the money
	prima!	great!
	pro	per
das	**Problem(e)**	problem
	kein Problem	no problem
der	**Prospekt(e)**	leaflet, brochure
der	**Pulli(s)/Pullover(-)**	pullover
	pünktlich	punctual
die	**Puppe(n)**	doll, puppet
die	**Purzelwörter** (pl)	jumbled words

Q

	qm/Quadratmeter	square metre
	Quatsch!	nonsense!

R

das	**Rad(¨er)**	bicycle
das	**Radfahren**	cycling
der	**Radiorekorder(-)**	ghetto blaster
die	**Radtour(en)**	cycle tour
der	**Rasierapparat(e)**	razor
das	**Rathaus(¨er)**	town hall
der	**Räuber(-)**	robber
der	**Rauch**	smoke
die	**Realschule(n)**	secondary school
	rechnen	to count, do arithmetic
	recht(er/e/es)	right
	rechts	on the right
der	**Refrain**	refrain, chorus
die	**Regel(n)**	rule
der	**Regenmantel(¨)**	raincoat
das	**reicht**	that's enough
die	**Reihenfolge**	order, sequence
das	**Reinigungsmittel**	detergent
die	**Reise(n)**	journey
das	**Reisebüro(s)**	travel agency
	reisen	to travel
der	**Reiseverlauf**	course of the journey
das	**Reiten**	riding
	reiten	to ride
die	**Reservierung(en)**	reservation
der	**Rest(e)**	remains
das	**Restaurant(s)**	restaurant
	richtig	correct
die	**Richtung(en)**	direction
	riesig	huge, gigantic
der	**Ring(e)**	ring
der	**Rock(¨e)**	skirt
das	**Rollschuhlaufen**	roller skating
	rot	red
die	**Rückenschmerzen** (pl)	backache
die	**Rückfahrkarte(n)**	return ticket
die	**Rückfahrt(en)**	return journey
der	**Rückflug(¨e)**	return flight
die	**Rückflugkarte(n)**	return plane ticket
die	**Ruhe**	peace, quiet
	ruhig	peaceful, calm
	rumänisch	Romanian
	rund	round
die	**Rundfahrt(en)**	circular tour

S

der	**Saal(Säle)**	hall, large room
die	**Sachen** (pl)	things
der	**Saft**	juice
	sagen	to say
ich	**sagte**	I said (from **sagen**)
ich	**sah**	I saw (from **sehen**)
die	**Sahne**	cream
die	**Saison**	season (e.g. football season)
die	**Salbe(n)**	ointment
	sammeln	to collect
der	**Samstag**	Saturday
der	**Sand**	sand
die	**Sandale(n)**	sandal
der	**Satz(¨e)**	sentence
	sauber	clean
die	**S-Bahn**	suburban railway
die	**S-Bahnhaltestelle(n)**	suburban railway station
die	**Schachtel(n)**	cardboard box
	schade	a pity
der	**Schäferhund(e)**	German shepherd dog
der	**Schal(e)**	scarf
der	**Schalter(-)**	counter; ticket office
der	**Schaukelstuhl(¨e)**	rocking chair
	scheinen	to shine; to seem
	schenken	to give as a present
	schick	smart, trendy
	schicken	to send
	schießen	to shoot
das	**Schiff(e)**	ship
die	**Schiffsreise(n)**	voyage
der	**Schinken**	ham
der	**Schlafanzug(¨e)**	pyjamas
	schlafen	to sleep
	schlank	slim
	schlecht	bad
das	**Schließfach(¨er)**	locker
	schließlich	finally
	schlimm	bad, serious
der	**Schlittschuh(e)**	skate
das	**Schloss(Schlösser)**	castle
der	**Schlüssel(-)**	key
	schmatzen	to smack one's lips
die	**Schmerztablette(n)**	pain killer
der	**Schmuck**	jewelry
	schmutzig	dirty
	schnappen	to grab

schnell fast
der Schnellimbiss snack bar
die Schnittwunde(n) cut
der Schnupfen(-) cold
die Schokolade chocolate
schon already
schön beautiful, pretty, nice
Schottland Scotland
schreiben to write
die Schreibwaren (pl) stationery
der Schuh(e) shoe
das Schuhgeschäft(e) shoe shop
die Schulaufgaben (pl) homework
die Schule(n) school
schulterlang shoulder-length
schwarz black
der Schwarzwald Black Forest
das Schwein(e) pig
die Schweiz Switzerland
schwer heavy; difficult
die Schwester(n) sister
das Schwimmbad(¨er) swimming pool
das Schwimmen swimming
schwimmen to swim
sechs six
der See(n) lake
die See(n) sea
seekrank seasick
die Seekrankheit seasickness
segeln to sail
sehen to see
die Sehenswürdigkeit(en) sight (worth seeing)
sehr very
seien Sie be (from sein)
Seien Sie so nett be so kind
die Seife soap
sein(e) his
sein to be
die Seite(n) side; page
auf der linken/rechten Seite on the left/right hand side
die Selbstbedienung self-service
selten seldom, rarely
der September September
sich himself, herself
Sie you (formal)
sie she; her (Acc); they, them (Acc)
sieben seven
sieh! look! (from sehen)
er/sie/es sieht he/she/it sees (from sehen)
das sind those are
singen to sing
sitzen to sit
das Ski(er) ski
das Skifahren/Skilaufen skiing

so so; this way
die Socke(n) sock
das Sofa(s) sofa
sofort at once
sogar even
der Sohn(¨e) son
sollen to have to
der Sommer(-) summer
der Sommerflugplan(¨e) summer flight timetable
das Sonderangebot(e) special offer
die Sonne(n) sun
sich sonnen to sunbathe
der Sonnenbrand(¨e) sunburn
das Sonnenlicht sunlight
der Sonntag Sunday
sonntags on Sundays
sonst otherwise
die Sorge(n) worry
mach dir keine Sorgen don't worry
Spanien Spain
spanisch Spanish
sparen to save
der Spaß joke, fun
viel Spaß! have fun!
spät late
spazieren gehen to go for a walk
der Specht(e) woodpecker
der Speisewagen(-) dining car
der Spiegel(-) mirror
das Spiegelbild(er) reflection
spielen to play
das Spielfeld(er) playing field
die Spielware(n) toy
der Sport sport
der Sportartikel(-) piece of sports equipment
die Sportausrüstung(en) sports kit
das Sportgeschäft(e) sports shop
die Sporthalle(n) sports hall
der/die Sportlehrer/in sports teacher
sportlich fond of sport, athletic
der Sportplatz(¨e) sports ground
der Spray(s) spray
die Sprechblase(n) speech bubble
sprechen to speak
die Spülmaschine(n) dishwasher
das Staatsballett state ballet
das Stadion(Stadien) stadium
die Stadt(¨e) town
die Stadthalle(n) civic hall
die Stadtmauer(n) town wall
die Stadtmitte(n) town centre
der Stadtplan(¨e) town map
die Stadtrundfahrt(en) tour of the town

das Stadtzentrum(-zentren) town centre
stecken to put (into)
stehen to stand
stellen to put (upright)
Fragen stellen to ask questions
der Stellplatz(¨e) space (at camping site)
die Stereoanlage(n) stereo equipment
die Stiefmutter(¨) stepmother
die Stiefschwester(n) stepsister
der Stiefvater(¨) stepfather
das stimmt that's right
stinklangweilig deadly boring
der Stock floor, storey
das Stofftier(e) soft toy (animal)
der Storch(¨e) stork
der Strand(¨e) beach
der Strandkorb(ë) wicker beach chair
die Straße(n) street
die Straßenbahn(en) tram
mit der Straßenbahn by tram
das Straßenschild(er) road sign
streng strict
der Strohhut(¨e) straw hat
die Strumpfhose(n) tights
das Stück(e) piece
der Student(en) student (boy)
die Studentin(nen) student (girl)
die Stunde(n) hour; lesson
stürmisch windy, rough
suchen to look for
im Süden in the south
der Supermarkt(¨e) supermarket
das Surfen surfing
surfen to go surfing
sympathisch kind, nice

T

der Tabak tobacco
die Tabelle(n) table, chart
die Tablette(n) tablet
die Tafel(n) blackboard; block (chocolate)
der Tag(e) day
der Tagestarif daily rate
täglich daily
die Tankstelle(n) petrol station
die Tante(n) aunt
das Tanzen dancing
tanzen to dance
die Tasche(n) pocket, bag
das Taschengeld pocket money
der Taschenrechner(-) pocket calculator
tausend thousand

der **Tee** tea
der **Teenager(-)** teenager
der **Teil(e)** part
teilen to share, divide
das **Telefon(e)** telephone
das **Telefongespräch(e)** telephone conversation
die **Telefonnummer(n)** telephone number
Tennis tennis
der **Tennisball("e)** tennis ball
die **Tennishalle(n)** indoor tennis court
der **Tennisplatz("e)** tennis court
der **Teppich(e)** carpet
der **Terminkalender(-)** diary
teuer expensive, dear
der **Text(e)** text, words
die **Themse-Metropole** Thames metropolis
die **Tiefkühlkost** frozen food
das **Tier(e)** animal
das **Tierheim(e)** animal home
der **Tisch(e)** table
Tischtennis table tennis
die **Tochter(")** daughter
der **Toilettenraum("e)** toilet area
toll! great!, marvellous!
die **Tomate(n)** tomato
die **Tomatensuppe(n)** tomato soup
total complete(ly)
der **Tourist(en)** tourist (male)
die **Touristik** tourism
die **Touristin(nen)** tourist (female)
die **Tournee(n)** tour
tragen to carry; to wear
der **Trainingsanzug("e)** tracksuit
treffen to meet
der **Treffpunkt** meeting place
treiben to do (sport)
Wassersport treiben to do water sports
der **Trimm-dich-Pfad(e)** keep-fit trail
trinken to drink
der **Tropfen(-)** drop
tschüss! cheerio, 'bye!
das **T-Shirt(s)** T-shirt
die **Tube(n)** tube
tun to do
es tut mir Leid I'm sorry
der **Turnschuh(e)** training shoe
die **Tüte(n)** bag
der **Typ(en)** character, chap

U

die **U-Bahn** the underground
die **U-Bahn-Station** underground station
üben to practise
über (+ Acc/Dat) over; about
überall everywhere
die **Überfahrt(en)** crossing
die **Übernachtung(en)** night's stay
überqueren to cross
die **Uhr(en)** clock
um (+ Acc) round
der **Umkleideraum("e)** changing room
umso größer so much the bigger
um/steigen to change (tram, bus, etc)
umweltfreundlich good for the environment, green
unbedingt definitely
und and
unheimlich awfully, tremendously
die **Universität(en)** university
unordentlich untidy
uns us
unser(e) our
unten below, downstairs
unter (+ Acc/Dat) under
das **Untergeschoss** basement
die **Unterhose(n)** pants
der **Unterricht** lessons, instruction
der **Urlaub** leave
der **Urlaubsplan("e)** holiday plan
die **Urlaubsreise(n)** holiday trip
die **Urlaubszeit(en)** holiday time
das **Urlaubsziel(e)** holiday destination

V

der **Vater(")** father
Vati Dad
der **Vegetarier(-)** vegetarian
verehrt respected, dear
verfügen über (+ Acc) to have at one's disposal
die **Verfügung** disposal
zur freien Verfügung to use as you like
das **Verkehrsamt** tourist information office
das **Verkehrsmittel(-)** means of transport
das **Verkehrsnetz** communications network

verkehrt wrong, wrong way round
die **Verletzung(en)** injury
vermissen to miss (person)
verpassen to miss (train, etc)
verrückt crazy, mad
die **Verspätung** delay
der Zug hat Verspätung the train is late
verstehen to understand
der **Verwandte(n)** relation
die **Videokamera(s)** video camera
die **Videokassette(n)** video cassette
viel much, a lot
viele many
vielleicht perhaps
vierjährig four year old
das **Viertel(-)** quarter
vierzehn fourteen
die **Vogelscheuche(n)** scarecrow
der **Volkspark(s)** public park
Volleyball volleyball
von (+ Dat) from, of
vor (+ Acc/Dat) in front of, before
vorbei past
vorgestern the day before yesterday
die **Vorsaison** early season
die **Vorsicht** caution, care
der **Vorteil(e)** advantage

W

der **Wackelpudding** blancmange
der **Wagen(-)** car
wählen to choose
während (+ Gen) during
Wales Wales
die **Wand("e)** wall
die **Wanderung(en)** hike
die **Wanderungsmöglichkeiten** (pl) hiking facilities
der **Wanderweg(e)** footpath
wann when
das **war** was (from **sein**)
wäre would be (from **sein**)
warm warm
die **Warmwasserdusche(n)** warm shower
warten (auf) (+ Acc) to wait (for)
der **Warteraum("e)** waiting room
warum why
was what
der **Wäschetrockner(-)** drier
die **Waschgelegenheit(en)** washing facilities
die **Waschmaschine(n)** washing machine

das	**Waschmittel(-)** detergent
der	**Waschraum(¨e)** washroom
das	**Wasser** water
der	**Wassersport** water sport
das	**WC(s)** toilet
der	**Weg(e)** way, path
	weg away, gone
	wegen (+ Gen) because of
er ist	**weggegangen** he has gone away (from **weg/gehen**)
der	**Wegweiser(-)** department store guide
	weh/tun to hurt
	es tut weh it hurts
	Weihnachten (pl) Christmas
der	**Wein(e)** wine
	weiß white
ich	**weiß** I know (from **wissen**)
	weit far
	weiter further
die	**Weiterfahrt** continued journey
	welch(er/e/es) which
die	**Welt(en)** world
	wem to whom
	wenig little
	wenn when; if
	wer who
die	**Werbung** advertising
	werden to become
das	**Wetter** weather
	wichtig important
	wie how, as, like
	wieder again
auf	**Wiedersehen** goodbye
	wieso why
	wie viel (wie viele) how much (how many)
ich	**will** I want (from **wollen**)
	willkommen welcome
	windig windy
der	**Winter** winter
	wir we
er/sie/es	**wird** he/she/it becomes, will (from **werden**)
	wo where
die	**Woche(n)** week
	wohin where to
	wohnen to live
der	**Wohnort(e)** home, place of residence
der	**Wohnwagen(-)** caravan
	wollen to want
die	**Wolljacke(n)** cardigan
das	**Wort(Wörter/Worte)** word
	wozu for what purpose, why
der	**Wucher** extortion, rip-off
	wund sore
das	**Wundermittel(-)** miracle cure
die	**Wunderstimme(n)** miracle voice
die	**Wurst(¨e)** sausage

Z

der	**Zahnarzt(¨e)** dentist
der	**Zahn(ë)** tooth
die	**Zahnpasta** toothpaste
die	**Zahnschmerzen** (pl) toothache
der	**Zauberberg** magic mountain
die	**Zebrastreifen** (pl) zebra stripes
	zehn ten
	zehntausend ten thousand
die	**Zeichenerklärung** explanation of symbols
	zeichnen to draw
die	**Zeit(en)** time
die	**Zeitschrift(en)** magazine
die	**Zeitung(en)** newspaper
das	**Zelt(e)** tent
der	**Zettel(-)** note; piece of paper
das	**Ziel(e)** destination
	ziemlich fairly, quite
	zollfrei duty-free
der	**Zoo(s)** zoo
	zu (+ Dat) to; too
	zuerst first
	zufrieden satisfied
der	**Zug(¨e)** train
	zu/lachen to smile at
	zurück back
	zusammen together
	zu viel too much
	zwanzig twenty
	zwei two
	zweihundert two hundred
	zweimal twice
das	**zweit(er/e/es)** second
	zwischen (+ Acc/Dat) between
	zwölf twelve

A

a ein(e)

to be **able** können

about über **(+ Acc)**
   about it darüber

absence note der Entschuldigungszettel(-)

absolute(ly) absolut

access road (motorway) die Einfahrt(en)

actually eigentlich

in **addition** dazu

address die Adresse(n)

adjective die Adjektive(n)

admiral der Admiral(e)

adult der Erwachsene(n)

advantage der Vorteil(e)

advertisement die Annonce(n)

advertising die Werbung

aeroplane das Flugzeug(e)

after nach
   after that danach

afternoon der Nachmittag(e)

again wieder

against gegen
   against it dagegen

age das Alter

airport der Flughafen(¨), der Flugplatz(¨e)

alcoholic alkoholisch

all alle(s)

allergic to allergisch (gegen)

allergy die Allergie(n)

allowed gestattet

almost fast

alone allein

already schon

also auch

always immer

I **am (from** sein) ich bin

America Amerika

and und

animal das Tier(e)

animal home das Tierheim(e)

anorak der Anorak(s)

to **answer** antworten, beantworten

answer die Antwort(en)

apart auseinander

appearance das Aussehen

apple der Apfel(¨)
   apple juice der Apfelsaft

approximately etwa

April der April

you **are (from** sein) du bist; ihr seid; Sie sind

area das Gebiet(e), die Gegend

arm der Arm(e)

arrival die Ankunft(¨e)

to **arrive** an/kommen

article der Artikel(-)

as als; wie

to **ask** bitten, fragen
   to ask questions Fragen stellen

aspirin die Aspirintablette(n)

at an **(+ Dat)**

B

athletic sportlich

August der August

aunt die Tante(n)

Australia Australien

Austria Österreich

away weg

awfully unheimlich

babysitter der Babysitter(-)

babysitting das Babysitten

back zurück
   at the back hinten
   backache die Rückenschmerzen **(pl)**

bad schlecht, schlimm
   bad luck das Pech

badminton Federball
   badminton raquet der Badmintonschläger(-)

bag die Tasche(n), die Tüte(n)

bakery die Bäckerei(en)

banana die Banane(n)

bank die Bank(en)

bar die Bar(s)

barbecue die Grillparty

basement das Untergeschoss

bath towel das Badetuch(¨er)

bathing cap die Bademütze(n)

bathing trunks die Badehose(n)

to **be** sein
   be so kind Seien Sie so nett

beach der Strand(¨e)

I can't **bear him** ich kann ihn nicht leiden

beautiful schön

because denn

because of aufgrund, wegen **(+ Gen)**

to **become** werden
   he becomes er wird

bed das Bett(en)
   bed linen die Bettwäsche

been (from sein) gewesen

beer das Bier(e)
   beer sausage die Bierwurst(¨e)

before vor **(+ Acc/Dat)**

to **begin** beginnen

beginning der Beginn

behind hinter **(+ Acc/Dat)**

to **believe** glauben

below unten

besides außerdem

best best(er/e/es)
   best of all am liebsten
   all the best alles Gute

better besser

between zwischen **(+ Acc/Dat)**

bicycle das Fahrrad(¨er), das Rad(¨er)

big groß

bikini der Bikini(s)

birthday der Geburtstag(e)
   birthday card die Geburtstagskarte(n)
   birthday party die Geburtstagsfeier(n)

biscuit(s) der Keks(e); die Backwaren **(pl)**

a **bit** ein bisschen

black schwarz
   Black Forest der Schwarzwald

blackboard die Tafel(n)

blancmange der Wackelpudding

block (chocolate) die Tafel(n)

blonde blond

blouse die Bluse(n)

blue blau

boat hire der Bootsverleih

book das Buch(¨er)
   book shop die Buchhandlung(en)

border die Grenze(n)

boring langweilig

both beides

bottle die Flasche(n)

bought (from kaufen) gekauft

bowling das Kegeln
   bowling alley die Kegelbahn(en)

box der Kasten(¨)

boy der Junge(n)

bra der BH

brain das Gehirn

bread das Brot(e)

to **break** brechen

breakfast das Frühstück

breeze die Brise(n)

in **brief** in Kürze

to **bring** bringen

British britisch

brochure die Broschüre(n), der Prospekt(e)

broken (from brechen) gebrochen

brother der Bruder(¨)
   brothers and sisters die Geschwister **(pl)**

brown braun

bunch of flowers der Blumenstrauß(¨e)

bus der Bus(se)
   bus route die Buslinie(n)
   bus station der Busbahnhof(¨e)
   bus stop die Bushaltestelle(n)
   bus timetable der Busfahrplan(¨e)

but aber

butcher's shop die Metzgerei(en)

butter die Butter

to **buy** kaufen

by bei **(+ Dat)**; **(transport)** mit **(+ Dat)**

C

café das Café(s)

cake der Kuchen(-)
   cake shop die Konditorei(en)

to **call** nennen

to be **called** heißen

camel das Kamel(e)

camera der Fotoapparat(e)

camper van der Campingbus(se)

camping der Camping

campsite der Campingplatz(¨e)

campsite rule die Campingplatzregel(n)

I/you can (from können) ich kann/ du kannst

can die Dose(n)

canal der Kanal(¨e)

capital city die Hauptstadt(¨e)

capsule die Kapsel(n)

car das Auto(s), der Wagen(-)

car park der Parkplatz(¨e)

car wash der Autowaschplatz(¨e)

caravan der Wohnwagen(-)

card die Karte(n)

cardboard box die Schachtel(n)

cardigan die Wolljacke(n)

carpet der Teppich(e)

carried (from tragen) getragen

carrot die Karotte(n)

to carry tragen

cash bar

cassette die Kassette(n)

castle das Schloss(Schlösser)

cathedral der Dom(e)

caution die Vorsicht

CD-player der CD-Spieler(-)

to celebrate feiern

celebrated gefeiert

chain game das Kettenspiel(e)

to change (tram, bus, etc) um/steigen

changing room der Umkleideraum(¨e)

character der Typ(en)

cheap billig

cheese der Käse

chemist's die Drogerie(n); die Apotheke(n)

child das Kind(er)

children's pool das Kinderschwimmbecken(-)

chocolate die Praline(n), die Schokolade

to choose wählen

chorus der Refrain

Christmas Weihnachten (pl)

church die Kirche(n)

cinema das Kino(s)

civic hall die Stadthalle(n)

class die Klasse(n)

class teacher der/die Klassenlehrer/in

class trip die Klassenfahrt(en)

classwork die Klassenarbeit(en)

clean sauber

clear klar

clock die Uhr(en)

closed (from schließen) geschlossen

clothes die Kleider (pl) (slang) die Klamotten (pl)

clothes shop das Kleidergeschäft(¨e)

coffee der Kaffee

coke die Cola(s)

cold der Schnupfen(-), die Erkältung(en); kalt

to collect sammeln

collection (of post) die Leerung(en)

colour die Farbe(n)

colourful bunt

to come kommen

come gekommen

to come with someone mit/kommen

that comes to das macht

comfortable bequem

communications network das Verkehrsnetz

compact disc die CD(s)

complete(ly) total

complicated kompliziert

comprehensive school die Gesamtschule(n)

computer der Computer(-)

computer club der Computerklub(s)

computer game das Computerspiel(e)

concert das Konzert(e)

confirmation die Konfirmation(en)

to consist of bestehen aus

conversation das Gespräch(e)

to cook kochen

correct richtig

cosmetics die Kosmetik

to cost kosten

cough sweet der Hustenbonbon(s)

I could, was able (from können) ich konnte

count der Graf(en)

to count, do arithmetic rechnen

counter der Schalter(-)

country das Land(¨er)

couple das Paar(e)

of course natürlich

cousin die Kusine(n); der Cousin(s)

covered belegt

crazy verrückt

cream die Sahne

to cross überqueren

crossing die Überfahrt(en)

crowd die Menge(n)

curly lockig

cut die Schnittwunde(n)

to cycle Rad fahren

cycle path der Fahrradweg(e)

cycle tour die Radtour(en)

cycling das Radfahren

 D

Dad Vati

daily täglich

daily rate der Tagestarif

dairy product das Milchprodukt(e)

to dance tanzen

danced getanzt

dancing das Tanzen

dark dunkel

daughter die Tochter(¨)

day der Tag(e)

deadly boring stinklangweilig

dear lieb; teuer; (in letters) Liebe/Lieber; geehrt(e/r)

December der Dezember

definitely bestimmt, unbedingt

delay die Verspätung

delicatessen die Feinkost

dentist der Zahnarzt(¨e)

department store das Kaufhaus(¨er)

store guide der Wegweiser(-)

departure die Abfahrt(en)

to describe beschreiben

destination das Ziel(e)

detergent das Reinigungs- mittel(-), das Waschmittel(-)

diagram das Diagramm(e)

dialogue der Dialog(e)

diary der Terminkalender(-)

to dictate diktieren

difficult schwer

dining car der Speisewagen(-)

direct direkt

direction die Richtung(en)

dirty schmutzig

disadvantage der Nachteil(e)

disco die Disko(s)

dishwasher die Spülmaschine(n)

disposal die Verfügung

distant entfernt

district das Gebiet(e), die Gegend

to do tun, machen; (sport) treiben

doctor der Arzt(¨e); der Doktor(en)

dog der Hund(e)

doll die Puppe(n)

done getan, gemacht

downstairs unten

to draw zeichnen

dress das Kleid(er)

drier der Wäschetrockner(-)

drink das Getränk(e)

to drink trinken

drop der Tropfen(-)

drunk (from trinken) getrunken

dune die Düne(n)

during während (+ Gen)

duty-free zollfrei

E

each jed(er/e/es)
ear das Ohr(en)
  ear ring der Ohrring(e)
  earache die Ohrenschmerzen
early früh
in the **east** im Osten
easy einfach
to **eat** essen
eaten (from essen) gegessen
either ... or ... entweder ...
  oder ...
emergency exit der
  Notausgang("e)
empty leer
to **empty** leeren
to **enclose** bei/legen
end das Ende(n)
English (lang) Englisch; **(adj)**
  englisch
  Englishman/woman
  der Engländer(-)/
  die Engländerin(nen)
enough genug
  that's enough das reicht
entrance der Eingang("e)
  entrance charge der
  Eintritt(e)
environmentally friendly
  umweltfreundlich
equal egal
even sogar
evening der Abend(e)
  in the evening abends
  evening dress das
  Abendkleid(er)
ever je
every jed(er/e/es)
everything alle(s)
everywhere überall
exact(ly) genau
  for example zum Beispiel
money **exchange** der Geldwechsel
excursion der Ausflug("e)
excuse die Ausrede(n)
to **excuse** entschuldigen
exercise book das Heft(e)
exit die Ausfahrt(en); der
  Ausgang("e)
expensive teuer
explanation of symbols die
  Zeichenerklärung
eye das Auge(n)

F

face das Gesicht(er)
factory die Fabrik(en)
fair fair
fairly ziemlich
to **fall** fallen
fallen (from fallen) gefallen
family die Familie(n)
  family visit der Familienbesuch
fantastic fantastisch
far weit, fern
fashion die Mode(n)
fast schnell

fat dick
father der Vater(")
favourite Lieblings-
fear of flying die Flugangst
February der Februar
to **feel** fühlen
fellow der Kerl(e)
fellow pupil der Mitschüler(-),
  die Mitschülerin(nen)
ferry die Fähre(n)
  by ferry mit der Fähre
to **fetch** holen
fever das Fieber
a **few** ein paar
field das Feld(er)
film der Film(e)
finally schließlich
to **find** finden
fine, splendid fein
fire der Brand("e)
first erst(er/e/es); zuerst
  first class erste Klasse
to **fish** angeln
fish der Fisch(e)
fishing das Angeln
fit fit
to **fit** passen
flair der Pfiff
flight der Flug("e)
  flight timetable der
  Flugplan("e)
floor der Stock
  on the first floor
  im ersten Stock
  on the ground floor
  im Erdgeschoss
flower die Blume(n)
  flower pot der Blumentopf("e)
flown (from fliegen) geflogen
flu die Grippe
flute die Flöte(n)
to **fly** fliegen
following folgend
food (groceries) die
  Lebensmittel **(pl)**; **(meal)**
  das Essen
foot der Fuß("e)
  on foot zu Fuß
football der Fußball(bälle)
  federal football league
  die Bundesliga
  football boot
  der Fußballschuh(e)
  football match
  das Fußballspiel(e)
  football stadium das
  Fußballstadion(-stadien)
footpath der Wanderweg(e)
for für
foreign fremd
to **form** bilden
form das Formular(e)
France Frankreich
free kostenlos; frei
Friday der Freitag
friend die Freundin(nen), der
  Freund(e)

friendly freundlich
from ab; von **(+ Dat)**
  from it davon
in **front of** vor **(+ Acc/Dat)**
frontier die Grenze(n)
frozen food die Tiefkühlkost
fruit das Obst
fun der Spaß
  have fun! viel Spaß!
furnishings die Einrichtungen
  (pl)
furniture die Möbel (pl)
further weiter

G

gap die Lücke(n)
garden der Garten(")
genius das Genie(s)
German shepherd dog
  der Schäferhund(e)
Germany Deutschland
to **get, receive** bekommen
ghetto blaster der Radio-
  rekorder(-)
girl das Mädchen(-), das Girl(s)
to **give** geben; **(as a present)**
  schenken
  he gives er gibt
given (from geben) gegeben
gladly gern(e)
glass das Glas("er)
pair of **glasses** die Brille(n)
glove der Handschuh(e)
gnat die Mücke(n)
to **go** gehen
to **go out** aus/gehen
to **go away** weg/gehen
goldfish der Goldfisch(e)
gone (from gehen) gegangen;
  weg
he has **gone away (from** weg/gehen)
  er ist weggegangen
good gut
  Good heavens! Mensch!
  Good morning! Guten
  Morgen!
goodbye auf Wiedersehen,
  tschüss
to **grab** schnappen
graffiti die Graffiti
gramme das Gramm
grandfather der Großvater("),
  der Opa
grandmother die
  Großmutter("), die Oma
great! prima!, toll!
green grün
greeting der Gruß("e)
grey grau
group die Gruppe(n), die
  Clique(n)
  group photo
  das Gruppenfoto(s)
  group work
  die Gruppenarbeit
to **guess** erraten
guest der Gast("e)
guitar die Gitarre(n)

H

had (from haben**)** ich hatte
hair das Haar(e)
hairy haarig
half halb
hall der Saal(Säle)
ham der Schinken
Hamburger der Hamburger(-)
hammer der Hammer(¨)
hand die Hand(¨e)
happiness die Glückseligkeit
hard working fleißig
he **has (from** haben**)** er hat
to **hate** hassen
to **have** haben
to **have to** müssen; sollen
hay fever der Heuschnupfen
he er
head der Kopf(¨e)
headache die Kopfschmerzen
headphone der Kopfhörer(-)
healing power die Heilkraft
healthy gesund
to **hear** hören
heard (from hören**)** gehört
heated beheizt
heavy schwer
hello! hallo!, grüß dich!
help die Hilfe
to **help** helfen
  he helps er hilft
her (Acc) sie; **to her (Dat)** ihr; ihr(e)
here hier
herself sich
high hoch
hike die Wanderung(en)
him ihn **(Acc)**; **to him** ihm **(Dat)**
himself sich
his sein(e)
history die Geschichte(n)
hit parade die Hitparade
hobby das Hobby(s)
holidays die Ferien **(pl)**
  holiday destination das Urlaubsziel(e)
  holiday plan der Urlaubsplan(¨e)
  holiday time die Urlaubszeit(en)
  holiday trip die Urlaubsreise(n)
home der Wohnort(e)
  at home zu Hause
  (to) home nach Hause
homework die Hausaufgaben **(pl)**, die Schulaufgaben **(pl)**
honest ehrlich
honey der Honig
I **hope** hoffentlich
horrible fies
hospital das Krankenhaus(¨er)
hotel das Hotel(s)
hour die Stunde(n)
house das Haus(¨er)
  at the house of bei **(+ Dat)**

how wie
  how are you? wie geht's?
  how much (how many) wie viel (wie viele)
however doch
huge riesig
to **hurt** weh/tun
  it hurts es tut weh

I

I ich
ice cream das Eis
ice cream parlour die Eisdiele(n)
idea die Idee(n); die Ahnung
  no idea! keine Ahnung!
ideal ideal
if wenn
ill krank
illness die Krankheit(en)
image das Image
important wichtig
in in **(+ Acc/Dat)**
inclusive inkl.(= inklusiv)
information die Auskunft(¨e), die Information(en)
injury die Verletzung(en)
to **inspect** besichtigen
to **interest** interessieren
into in **(+ Acc)**
to **invent** erfinden
invitation die Einladung(en)
iron das Bügeleisen(-)
he/she/it **is** er/sie/es ist
island die Insel(n)
it es; sie; er
Italy Italien
item of clothing das Kleidungsstück(e)

J

jacket die Jacke(n)
jam die Konfitüre(n)
January der Januar
jar das Glas(¨er)
jeans die Jeans **(pl)**
jelly bears die Gummibärchen
jewelry der Schmuck
job der Job(s), die Arbeit(en)
joke der Spaß
journey die Fahrt(en), die Reise(n)
juice der Saft
July der Juli
June der Juni
just bloß
  just a moment! Moment mal!

K

keep-fit trail der Trimm-dich-Pfad(e)
key der Schlüssel(-)
kilogramme das Kilo(s)
kilometre der Kilometer(-)
kind lieb
kiosk der Kiosk(e)
to **know (a person)** kennen; **(a fact)** wissen
I **know (from** wissen**)** ich weiß

L

to **label** beschriften
lady die Dame(n)
lake der See(n)
lamp die Lampe(n)
to **last** dauern
last letzt(er/e/es)
late spät
  the train is late der Zug hat Verspätung
to **laugh** lachen
leaflet die Broschüre(n)
to **learn** lernen
leather jacket die Lederjacke(n)
leave der Urlaub
left link(er/e/es)
  on the left links
  on the left hand side auf der linken Seite
left luggage office die Gepäckaufbewahrung
leg das Bein(e)
lesson(s) die Stunde(n); der Unterricht
Let's go! Los!
letter der Brief(e)
letter-box der Briefkasten(¨)
library die Bibliothek(en)
to **lie** liegen
life das Leben(-)
light brown hellbraun
lightning der Blitz
to **like** mögen
  I'd like ich möchte
  you would like du möchtest
  I like ich mag
  I like ice cream ich esse gern Eis
  I like it es gefällt mir
like wie
list die Liste(n)
  list of hotels die Hotelliste(n)
litre der Liter(-)
little wenig
a **little** ein bisschen
to **live** wohnen
loaf das Brot(e)
locker das Schließfach(¨er)
long lang
  for a long time lange
to **look** sehen, gucken; **(appear)** aus/sehen
look! (from sehen**)** sieh!
to **look at** an/sehen
to **look for** suchen
looked for (from suchen**)** gesucht
lost property office das Fundbüro(s)
loud laut
luck das Glück
luggage trolley der Kofferkuli(s)

M

mad verrückt
magazine die Zeitschrift(en)
make-up das Make-up
man der Mann(¨er), der Herr(en)
many viele
  how many wie viele
map die Landkarte(n)
March der März
margarine die Margarine
mark die DM (Deutschmark), die Mark(-)
market der Markt(¨e)
market place der Marktplatz(¨e)
Mars bar der Marsriegel(-)
maths die Mathe
what's the **matter?** was ist los?
May der Mai
I/you **may (from** dürfen**)** ich darf/du darfst
me mich **(Acc)**; to me mir **(Dat)**
means of transport das Verkehrsmittel(-)
meat das Fleisch
medicine das Medikament(e)
medium length mittellang
medium sized mittelgroß
to **meet** treffen
meeting place der Treffpunkt
member of family das Familienmitglied(er)
met (from treffen**)** getroffen
metal das Metal(e)
metre das Meter(-)
microphone der Mikrofon
midday der Mittag
in the **middle of** mitten in **(+ Dat)**
milk die Milch
milkshake der Milkshake
minigolf der Minigolf
miniskirt der Minirock(¨e)
minute die Minute(n)
mirror der Spiegel(-)
to **miss (person)** vermissen; **(train, etc)** verpassen
to be **missing** fehlen
modern modern
moment der Moment(e)
  just a moment! Moment mal!
Monday der Montag
money das Geld
month der Monat(e)
moped das Mofa(s)
more mehr
morning der Morgen(-)
most die meisten
mostly meistens
mother die Mutter(¨)
motorway die Autobahn(en)
mountain der Berg(e)
mouse die Maus(¨e)
Mr Herr
Mrs. Frau

much viel
  how much wie viel
muddle das Durcheinander
multi-storey car park das Parkhaus(¨er)
Mum Mutti
museum das Museum(Museen)
music die Musik

N

I **must, have to (from** müssen**)** ich muss
my mein(e)

naked nackt
name der Name(n)
nearby in der Nähe
necklace die Halskette(n)
to **need** brauchen
negative negativ
never nie
new neu
newspaper die Zeitung(en)
next nächst(er/e/es)
nice nett; sympathisch; schön
night die Nacht(¨e)
  night's stay die Übernachtung(en)
  night-club die Bar(s)
no nein, nee **(colloquial)**; kein(e)
nobody niemand
nonsense! Quatsch!
normally normalerweise
North Germany Norddeutschland
North Sea die Nordsee
in the **north** im Norden
not nicht
  not at all gar nicht
  not until erst
  not yet noch nicht
note der Zettel(-)
nothing nichts
  nothing special nichts Besonderes
November der November
now jetzt
number die Nummer(n)

O

observation tower der Aussichtsturm(¨e)
October der Oktober
of von **(+ Dat)**
office das Büro(s)
ointment die Salbe(n)
that's **OK** das geht
old alt
  old part of town die Altstadt(¨e)
Olympic centre das Olympiazentrum
Olympic stadium das Olympiastadion
on an **(+ Acc/Dat)**; auf **(+ Acc/Dat)**
once einmal
  once more nochmal

at **once** sofort
one ein(e); eins; man
  one and a half anderthalb
only nur; erst
onto an **(+ Acc)**; auf **(+ Acc)**
opera die Oper(n)
opinion die Meinung(en)
or oder
orchestra das Orchester(-)
order die Reihenfolge
other ander(er/e/es)
otherwise sonst
ouch! Aua!
our unser(e)
out of aus **(+ Dat)**
outside außerhalb
over über **(+ Acc/Dat)**
  over it darüber
  over there drüben
owl die Eule(n)
own eigen(er/e/es)

P

packet die Packung(en)
page die Seite(n)
pain killer die Schmerztablette(n)
pairwork die Partnerarbeit
pants die Unterhose(n)
parents die Eltern **(pl)**
park der Park(s)
part der Teil(e)
partner der Partner(-), die Partnerin(nen)
party die Party(s)
past vorbei
path der Weg(e)
peace die Ruhe
peaceful ruhig
pedestrian precinct die Fußgängerzone(n)
pencil der Bleistift(e)
people die Leute **(pl)**
per je; pro
  per person je Person
perfume das Parfüm
perhaps vielleicht
person der Mensch(en), die Person(en)
pet food die Haustiernahrung
petrol consumption der Benzinverbrauch
petrol station die Tankstelle(n)
photo das Foto(s)
photograph album das Fotoalbum(-alben)
picnic das Picknick
picture das Bild(er)
piece das Stück(e)
  piece of sports equipment der Sportartikel(-)
pig das Schwein(e)
pillow das Kopfkissen(-)
pistol die Pistole(n)
a **pity** schade
pizza die Pizza(s)

	plan der Plan(¨e)
to	**plan** planen
	plant die Pflanze(n)
	plaster das Pflaster(-)
	platform das Gleis(e), der Bahnsteig(e)
to	**play** spielen
	playground der Kinderspielplatz(¨e)
	playing field das Spielfeld(er)
	please bitte
to	**please** gefallen
	pocket calculator der Taschenrechner(-)
	pocket die Tasche(n)
	pocket money das Taschengeld
	poem das Gedicht(e)
	policeman der Polizist(en)
	polo-necked shirt das Polohemd(en)
	poor arm
	pop concert das Popkonzert(e)
	pop group die Popgruppe(n)
	pop star der Popstar(s)
	positive positiv
	post die Post
	postcard die Postkarte(n)
	poster das Poster(-)
	potato die Kartoffel(n)
	pound das Pfund(-)
	practical(ly) praktisch
to	**practise** üben
I	**prefer to fly** ich fliege lieber
	preferably lieber
	present das Geschenk(e)
	present, there dabei
	pretty schön
	price der Preis(e)
	price list die Preisliste(n)
	primary school die Grundschule(n)
	printer der Drucker(-)
	prison das Gefängnis(se)
	private car der PKW(s)
	problem das Problem(e)
	pullover der Pulli(s), der Pullover(-)
	punctual pünktlich
	purchase der Einkauf(¨e)
	purse das Portmonee(s)
to	**put (into)** stecken; **(onto)** legen; **(upright)** stellen
	pyjamas der Schlafanzug(¨e)

Q

	quarter das Viertel(-)
	question die Frage(n)
	quite ganz; ziemlich

R

	rabbit das Kaninchen(-)
	raincoat der Regenmantel(¨)
	razor der Rasierapparat(e)
to	**reach** erreichen
to	**read** lesen
	he reads er liest
	read! lies!
	reader der Leser(-)

	reading das Lesen
	ready fertig
	ready-made meal das Fertiggericht(e)
	really eigentlich
	reasonable preiswert
to give	**reasons for** begründen
to	**receive** bekommen
to	**recommend** empfehlen
	recovery die Besserung
	red rot
	reduction die Ermäßigung(en)
	reflection das Spiegelbild(er)
	registration die Anmeldung(en)
	relation der Verwandte(n)
	remains der Rest(e)
to	**replace** ersetzen
to	**report** melden
to	**request** an/fordern
	reservation die Buchung(en), die Reservierung(en)
	respected verehrt
	restaurant das Restaurant(s)
	return flight der Rückflug(¨e)
	return journey die Rückfahrt(en)
	return ticket die Rückfahrkarte(n), hin und zurück
to	**ride** reiten
	riding das Reiten
that's	**right** das stimmt
	right recht(er/e/es)
	on the right rechts
	on the right hand side auf der rechten Seite
	ring der Ring(e)
that's a	**rip-off** das ist Wucher
	river der Fluss(Flüsse)
	road sign das Straßenschild(er)
	robber der Räuber(-)
	rock der Felsen(-)
	rocking chair der Schaukelstuhl(¨e)
	roll das Brötchen(-)
	roller skating das Rollschuhlaufen
	Romanian rumänisch
	rough stürmisch
	round rund; um **(+ Acc)**
	route (of bus) die Linie(n)
	rule die Regel(n)
to	**run** laufen

S

I	**said (from** sagen**)** ich sagte
to	**sail** segeln
the	**same** gleich
	it's all the same to me es ist mir egal
	sand der Sand
	sandal die Sandale(n)
	sandwich belegtes Brot
	satisfied zufrieden

	Saturday der Samstag
	sausage die Wurst(¨e)
to	**save** sparen
I	**saw (from** sehen**)** ich sah
to	**say** sagen
	scarecrow die Vogelscheuche(n)
	scarf der Schal(s)
	school die Schule(n)
	Scotland Schottland
	sea das Meer(e), die See(n)
	seasick seekrank
	seasickness die Seekrankheit
	season die Saison
	high season die Hauptsaison(s)
	seat der Platz(¨e)
	second zweit(er/e/es)
	secondary school die Realschule(n)
to	**see** sehen
	he sees er sieht
to	**seem** scheinen
	seen (from sehen**)** gesehen
	seldom selten
	self-service die Selbstbedienung
to	**send** schicken
	to send off ab/schicken
	sentence der Satz(¨e)
	September der September
	serious schlimm
	several times mehrmals
to	**share** teilen
	she sie
	shellfish, mussel die Muschel(n)
to	**shine** scheinen
	ship das Schiff(e)
	shirt das Hemd(en)
	shoe der Schuh(e)
	shoe shop das Schuhgeschäft(e)
to	**shoot** schießen
to	**shop** das Geschäft(e)
to	**shop** ein/kaufen
I go	**shopping** ich mache Einkäufe
	shopping list die Einkaufsliste(n)
	short kurz
	shoulder-length schulterlang
	shower die Dusche(n)
	shower die Dusche(n)
	side die Seite(n)
	sight die Sehenswürdigkeit(en)
	similar ähnlich
to	**sing** singen
	single (ticket) einfach
	sister die Schwester(n)
to	**sit** sitzen
to be	**situated** sich befinden
	size die Größe(n)
	skate der Schlittschuh(e)
	ski das Ski(er)
	skiing das Skifahren/ Skilaufen

to **skirt** der Rock(¨e)
to **sleep** schlafen
slept (from schlafen)
  geschlafen
slim schlank
small klein
smart schick
to **smile at** zu/lachen
smoke der Rauch
smooth glatt
snack bar der Schnellimbiss
so also; so
  so much the bigger
  umso größer
soap die Seife
sock die Socke(n)
sofa das Sofa(s)
soft(ly) leise
soft toy (animal) das
  Stofftier(e)
some einige
someone jemand
something etwas
  something special etwas
  Besonderes
sometimes manchmal
son der Sohn(¨e)
soon bald
sore wund
  sore throat
  die Halsschmerzen (pl)
Sorry! Entschuldigung!
  I'm sorry es tut mir Leid
in the **south** im Süden
souvenir das Andenken(-)
Spain Spanien
Spanish spanisch
to **speak** sprechen
special offer das
  Sonderangebot(e)
speech bubble die
  Sprechblase(n)
to **spend (money)** aus/geben
spoken (from sprechen)
  gesprochen
sport der Sport
  sports ground
  der Sportplatz(¨e)
  sports hall
  die Sporthalle(n)
  sports kit
  die Sportausrüstung(en)
  sports shop
  das Sportgeschäft(e)
spot der Pickel(-)
spray der Spray(s)
square der Platz(¨e)
square metre qm/
  Quadratmeter
squirrel das Eichhörnchen(-)
stadium das Stadion(Stadien)
stamp die Briefmarke(n)
to **stand** stehen
state ballet das Staatsballett
station der Bahnhof(¨e); der
  Hauptbahnhof(¨e)
stationery die Schreibwaren (pl)

to **stay** bleiben
stay der Aufenthalt
stayed (from bleiben)
  geblieben
stepfather der Stiefvater(¨)
stepmother die Stiefmutter(¨)
stepsister die
  Stiefschwester(n)
stereo equipment die
  Stereoanlage(n)
still noch
stomachache die
  Magenschmerzen (pl)
storey der Stock
stork der Storch(¨e)
story die Geschichte(n)
straight ahead geradeaus
straight gerade
straw hat der Strohhut(¨e)
street die Straße(n)
strict streng
striped gestreift
student der Student(en), die
  Studentin(nen)
stupid blöd, doof
suburban railway die S-Bahn
suddenly plötzlich
to **suffer** leiden
sufficient genügend
suit der Anzug(¨e)
to **suit** passen
suitable geeignet; passend
summer der Sommer(-)
sun die Sonne(n)
to **sunbathe** sich sonnen
sunburn der Sonnenbrand(¨e)
Sunday der Sonntag
  on Sundays sonntags
sunlight das Sonnenlicht
supermarket der
  Supermarkt(¨e)
surfing das Surfen
to go **surfing** surfen
to **swim** schwimmen
swimming das Schwimmen
  swimming pool
  das Schwimmbad(¨er)
  indoor swimming pool
  das Hallenbad(¨er)
  open-air pool
  das Freibad(¨er)
Switzerland die Schweiz

T

table der Tisch(e); die
  Tabelle(n)
table tennis Tischtennis
tablet die Tablette(n)
to **take** nehmen
to **take photographs**
  fotografieren
take-off der Abflug(¨e)
it **tasted good** es hat geschmeckt
tea der Tee
teacher der Lehrer(-), die
  Lehrerin(nen)
  German teacher

  der Deutschlehrer(-)
teenager der Teenager(-)
to **telephone** an/rufen
telephone das Telefon(e)
  telephone conversation
  das Telefongespräch(e)
  telephone number
  die Telefonnummer(n)
television das Fernsehen
  television (set)
  der Fernseher(-)
high **temperature** das Fieber
tennis Tennis
  tennis ball
  der Tennisball(¨e)
  tennis court
  der Tennisplatz(¨e)
  indoor tennis court
  die Tennishalle(n)
tent das Zelt(e)
terrible fürchterlich
text der Text(e)
than als
to **thank** danken
  thank you danke
  many thanks vielen Dank
that das; dass
the (m/f/n) der/die/das etc.
the day before yesterday
  vorgestern
their ihr(e)
them sie (Acc); **to them**
  ihnen (Dat)
then dann, anschließend
there da, dort; **(to) there**
  dahin, dorthin
there is/there are es gibt
they sie
thick dick
things die Sachen (pl)
to **think** denken; meinen
third dritt(er/e/es)
this, these dies(er/e/es)
three times dreimal
through durch
Thursday der Donnerstag
ticket die Fahrkarte(n)
  ticket machine
  der Fahrkartenautomat(en)
  ticket office der Schalter(-);
  die Kasse(n)
tights die Strumpfhose(n)
till die Kasse(n)
time das Mal; die Zeit(en)
timetable der Fahrplan(¨e)
tin die Dose(n)
  tinned food die Konserven
tired müde
to zu (+ Dat); nach (+ Dat); an
  (+ Acc)
  to and fro hin und her
tobacco der Tabak
today heute
together zusammen
toilet das WC(s), die Toilette(n)
  toilet area
  der Toilettenraum(¨e)

tomato die Tomate(n)
  tomato soup die Tomatensuppe(n)
tomorrow morgen
too auch; zu
  too much zu viel
tooth der Zahn(ë)
  toothache die Zahnschmerzen **(pl)**
  toothpaste die Zahnpasta
at the **top** oben
total amount die Gesamtsumme(n)
tour die Tournee(n)
  circular tour die Rundfahrt(en)
  tour of the town die Stadtrundfahrt(en)
tourism die Touristik
tourist der Tourist(en), die Touristin(nen)
tourist information office das Verkehrsamt
town centre das Stadtzentrum(-zentren), die Stadtmitte(n)
town die Stadt(¨e)
  town hall das Rathaus(¨er)
  town map der Stadtplan(¨e)
  town wall die Stadtmauer(n)
toy die Spielware(n)
tracksuit der Trainingsanzug(¨e)
train der Zug(¨e)
  by train mit der Bahn
training shoe der Turnschuh(e)
tram die Straßenbahn(en)
  by tram mit der Straßenbahn
travel agency das Reisebüro(s)
to **travel** reisen; fahren
travelled (from fahren) gefahren
tremendously unheimlich
trousers die Hose(n)
T-shirt das T-Shirt(s)
tub der Becher(-)
tube die Tube(n)
Tuesday der Dienstag
it's my **turn** ich bin dran
TV guide die Fernsehzeitung(en)
twice zweimal

U

uncle der Onkel(-)
under unter **(+ Acc/Dat)**
the **underground** die U-Bahn
  underground station die U-Bahnstation
to **understand** verstehen
unfortunately leider
unit die Einheit(en)
university die Universität(en)

untidy unordentlich
until bis
upstairs oben
us uns

V

vegetables das Gemüse
vegetarian der Vegetarier(-)
very sehr
video camera die Videokamera(s)
video cassette die Videokassette(n)
village das Dorf(¨er)
to **visit** besuchen
visit der Besuch(e)
volleyball Volleyball
voyage die Schiffsreise(n)

W

to **wait (for)** warten (auf) **(+ Acc)**
waiting room der Warteraum(¨e)
Wales Wales
to go for a **walk** spazieren gehen
wall die Wand(¨e), die Mauer(n)
to **want** wollen
  I want ich will
  do you want to …? hast du Lust …?
wardrobe der Kleiderschrank(¨e)
warm warm
was (from sein) war
washing machine die Waschmaschine(n)
washroom der Waschraum(¨e)
to **watch television** fern/sehen
watched TV (from fernsehen) ferngesehen
water das Wasser
  water sport der Wassersport
way der Weg(e)
we wir
to **wear** tragen
weather das Wetter
Wednesday der Mittwoch
week die Woche(n)
welcome willkommen
well gesund
  get well soon Gute Besserung
well na, na ja
Wellington boot der Gummistiefel(-)
he **went (from** gehen) er ging
what was
when als; wann; wenn
where wo, **(to)** wohin
which welch(er/e/es)
white weiß
who wer; **(m/f/n)** der/die/das
to **whom** wem
why warum; wieso; wozu

window das Fenster(-)
windy windig
wine der Wein(e)
winter der Winter
wish die Lust
  with best wishes (in letters) mit herzlichen Grüßen
with mit **(+ Dat)**; bei **(+ Dat)**
without ohne **(+ Acc)**
woman die Frau(en)
woodpecker der Specht(e)
word das Wort(Wörter/Worte)
to **work** arbeiten
work die Arbeit(en)
worked (from arbeiten) gearbeitet
world die Welt(en)
worn (from tragen) getragen
worry die Sorge(n)
  don't worry mach dir keine Sorgen
would be (from sein) wäre
wrist das Handgelenk(e)
  wrist watch die Armbanduhr(en)
to **write** schreiben
  to write down auf/schreiben
written (from schreiben) geschrieben
wrong falsch
  wrong way round verkehrt
  what's wrong with you? was fehlt dir?

Y

year das Jahr(e)
yellow gelb
yes ja
yesterday gestern
yoghurt der Jogurt(s)
you du; ihr; Sie; **(Acc)** dich; euch; Sie; **to you (Dat)** dir; euch; Ihnen
young jung
  young person der/die Jugendliche(n)
your dein(e); euer(e); Ihr(e)
youth centre das Jugendzentrum(-zentren)
youth club der Jugendklub(s)
youth hostel die Jugendherberge(n)

Z

zebra stripes die Zebrastreifen **(pl)**
zoo der Zoo(s)

Beantworte die Fragen.	*Answer the questions.*
Beschreib die Mädchen.	*Describe the girls.*
Beschrifte die Kleidungsstücke.	*Label the items of clothing.*
Diese Sätze sind durcheinander.	*These sentences are mixed up.*
Erfinde Dialoge/Namen.	*Invent conversations/names.*
Ersetz die Bilder mit den passenden Wörtern.	*Substitute the appropriate words for the pictures.*
Finde die richtigen Antworten.	*Find the right answers.*
Füll die Lücken/die Sprechblasen aus.	*Fill in the gaps/the speech bubbles.*
Hör (nochmal) gut zu.	*Listen carefully (again).*
Jetzt bist du dran!	*Now it's your turn.*
Kannst du andere … schreiben?	*Can you write other … ?*
Kannst du weitere Beispiele schreiben?	*Can you write some more examples?*
Kannst du andere Fragen stellen?	*Can you ask other questions?*
Lies den Brief/den Text/die Sätze/den Dialog.	*Read the letter/text/sentences/conversation.*
Mach Dialoge.	*Make up conversations.*
Mach eine Tabelle.	*Make a chart.*
Partnerarbeit.	*Pair work*
Richtig oder falsch?	*True or false?*
Schau im Wörterbuch nach.	*Look in the dictionary.*
Schlag in der Wörterliste nach.	*Look in the vocabulary list.*
Schreib ‚richtig' oder ‚falsch'.	*Write 'true' or 'false'.*
Schreib den Namen.	*Write the name.*
Schreib die (passenden) Namen/Preise auf.	*Write out the (correct) names/prices.*
Schreib die Sätze fertig.	*Complete the sentences.*
Schreib die Sätze in der richtigen Reihenfolge auf.	*Write out the sentences in the correct order.*
Schreib ein Zahlenrätsel/einen Brief.	*Write a number puzzle/a letter.*
Schreib folgende Sätze/die Antworten auf.	*Write out the following sentences/the answers.*
Sieh dir die Fotos/Bilder/Texte/den Schlüssel an.	*Look at the photos/pictures/texts/key.*
Sing mit.	*Sing along.*
Stell deinem Partner/deiner Partnerin Fragen.	*Ask your partner questions.*
Wähl den richtigen Satz/eine Person.	*Choose the correct sentence/a person.*
Was gehört zusammen?	*What belongs together?*
Was ist das?	*What is that?*
Was ist die Frage?	*What is the question?*
Was machst du (gern)?	*What do you (like to) do?*
Was meinst du?	*What do you think?*
Was passt wozu?	*What goes with what?*
Was sagen die Leute?	*What do the people say?*
Welche Antwort passt zu welcher Frage?	*Which answer matches which question?*
Welche Zahl ist das?	*What number is it?*
Welcher Text passt zu welchem Bild/Foto?	*Which text goes with which picture/photo?*
Welcher Titel passt am besten zu welchem Text?	*Which title goes best with which text?*
Welches Wort ist das?	*What word is it?*
Wer ist das/Nummer 1?	*Who is it/number 1?*
Wer sagt was?	*Who says what?*
Wer spricht?	*Who is speaking?*
Wie findest du sie?	*What do you think of them?*
Wie heißt … ?	*What is … called? How do you say … ?*
Wie ist das richtig?	*What is the right way/version?*
Wie ist die richtige Reihenfolge?	*What is the correct order?*
Wie schreibt man das richtig?	*How is this written correctly?*
Wie viel ist das (zusammen)?	*How much is that (altogether)?*
Wie viel macht das?	*How much does that come to?*
Wo sind diese Leute?	*Where are these people?*
Zeichne ein eigenes Poster/andere Bilder mit Text.	*Draw your own poster/other pictures with words.*

Dd dance Ee Ff

Jj Kk kangaroo Ll

Oo pail Pp Qq

umbrella Uu vegetables Vv

Yy Zz zebra

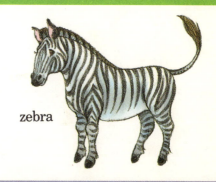

My
First
Muppet
Dictionary

My First Muppet Dictionary

Edited by Louise Gikow, Justine Korman, and Rita Rosenkranz

Designed by Sandra Forrest
Illustrated by Tom Cooke

Muppet Press

Special thanks to Lauren Attinello, Barbara Brenner,
Didi Charney, and Rick Pracher for their invaluable assistance,
and to Bruce McNally for his design concept.

This 1988 Muppet Press book is published by Longmeadow Press.

Manufactured in the United States of America

h g f e d c b a

A Letter from Jim Henson

One of the most important things we can do for our children is to encourage them to enjoy reading. I am therefore particularly delighted to introduce to you **My First Muppet Dictionary.**

This dictionary was designed to encourage young children to take an active interest in the words they speak and read. The language of the dictionary is simple and clear, and a special effort was made to define all the words in ways that children can easily understand. In addition, many of the words are woven into little illustrated "stories," making the dictionary fun to open at any point and just read.

Most of all, **My First Muppet Dictionary** was created in the hope that parents would look at it and read it *with* their children. If you encourage them to use a dictionary as they are learning to read, your children may well continue to do so as they grow up. This can improve their reading skills, strengthen their writing, and give them a strong appreciation of the English language.

I hope both you and your children will enjoy **My First Muppet Dictionary.**

Jim Henson

How to Use This Dictionary

Hi! This is Baby Kermit. Welcome to **My First Muppet Dictionary**! I'm here to tell you a little bit about how to use this book. It's really very easy.

To find a word, the first thing you have to do is figure out what the first letter of the word is. (Grown-ups can be very helpful with this.) Once you know, find the section for that letter of the alphabet. For instance, the word below is **pail,** so to find it, you'd have to find the section for **P.**

Now, suppose you wanted to know the meaning of the word **pail.** Follow me, and I'll show you what to look for!

1 First you have to find the word. Words in this dictionary are easy to find—they're nice and big, and they're always on the left side of the page.

2 This is another form of the word. In English, words can have lots of different forms. For instance, **pails** means more than one **pail.**

3 Now you can look at the picture. It will help you understand the word right away.

pail

pails

A **pail** is a container with a handle. Baby Piggy's **pail** is full of sand.

4 Here's the definition. It will tell you what the word means.

5 This sentence uses the word again so you can understand it even better.

See? I told you it was easy!

There's something else that's neat about this dictionary. Some of the pictures tell little stories or ask you questions. If you want to see what I mean, look at **whale** and **what.**

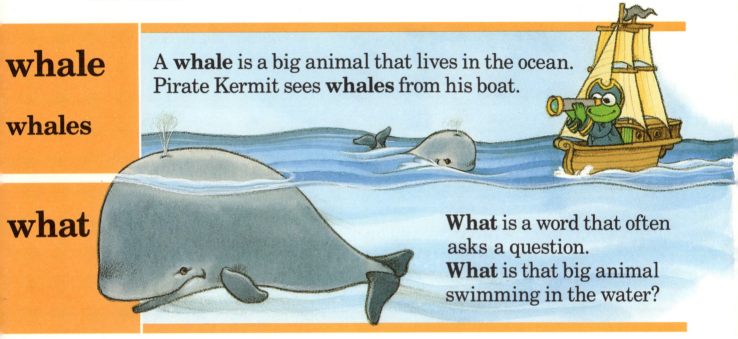

whale

whales

A **whale** is a big animal that lives in the ocean. Pirate Kermit sees **whales** from his boat.

what

What is a word that often asks a question. **What** is that big animal swimming in the water?

And just one more thing: Look at the definition under **whale** again. Do you want to know what the word **ocean** means? Well, just look it up under **O.** We've tried really hard to define most of the words that are in this book. (But if we've missed a few, just ask a grown-up to help.)

Well, I think I'm going to read a book myself right now. Have fun with the dictionary!

A Note to Grown-ups

This dictionary was carefully researched to include as many early vocabulary words as possible. We also attempted to include all the major definitions of words for children, so there sometimes are two definitions per word. But no dictionary says it all—and that's where *you* come in. We highly recommend using this dictionary with your child. You can help define additional words, and you can also point out to them those words that have more than one meaning in English. Learning about language can be a wonderful game—and you and your child can have a lot of fun using **My First Muppet Dictionary,** especially if you use it together.

A a

above

Above means over or higher than. There is a clock **above** Baby Kermit's head.

after

After is the opposite of before. Baby Piggy and Baby Kermit clean up **after** breakfast.

air

Air is what we breathe. **Air** is all around us.

airplane

airplanes

An **airplane** is a machine that flies. Baby Skeeter wants to fly an **airplane** when she grows up.

all

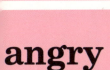

All means the whole of something.
Baby Animal has **all** the apples.

angry

Angry is being mad about something.
Baby Animal is **angry** because his
toy airplane is broken.

animal

animals

An **animal** is a living
thing that is not a plant.
An ape is an **animal**.

ankle

ankles

Your **ankle** joins your foot to your leg.
Simon says: Grab your **ankle**.

ant

ants

An **ant** is an insect.
An **ant** is not an aunt.
This **ant** lives in that anthill.

ape

apes

An **ape** is a smart animal that
looks like a big monkey.
Apes can walk on
two legs.
This **ape** is asleep.

apple
apples

An **apple** is a round fruit that grows on trees. Baby Animal has lots of **apples**.

arm
arms

Your **arm** is between your shoulder and your wrist. Simon says: Raise your **arms**.

ask
asks

You **ask** a question when you want to know something. Baby Kermit **asks** Animal how many apples he has.

asleep

When people and animals are not awake, they are **asleep**. Baby Gonzo dreams when he is **asleep**.

aunt
aunts

Your **aunt** is the sister of your father or mother. Your **aunts** and uncles are part of your family.

awake

When people and animals are not asleep, they are **awake**. Baby Gonzo is asleep, but Baby Animal is wide **awake**.

Bb

baby
babies

A **baby** is a very young person or animal. Animal is still a **baby**. He can't walk yet.

back

Back is the opposite of front. Your **back** is also a part of your body. Baby Gonzo is scratching his **back**.

bad

Bad is the opposite of good. It is **bad** to write on the walls.

bake
bakes

To **bake** is to cook something in an oven. The Swedish Chef **bakes** bread.

ball
balls

A **ball** is a round toy or thing. Baby Piggy plays with the **ball**.

barn
barns

A **barn** is a house for animals on a farm. Baby Gonzo takes the cow to the **barn**.

bath
baths

A **bath** is lots of water and soap to clean your body. Baby Kermit takes a **bath** with his boat.

beach
beaches

A **beach** is the sand by an ocean or lake. Baby Kermit and Baby Piggy play ball at the **beach**.

bean
beans

A **bean** is a vegetable. **Beans** can be green, yellow, red, white, or black.

bear
bears

A **bear** is a furry wild animal. This **bear** loves to eat honey.

bed

beds

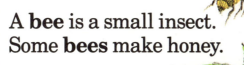

A **bed** is something soft to sleep in. Baby Gonzo puts Camilla into her **bed**.

bee

bees

A **bee** is a small insect. Some **bees** make honey.

before

Before is the opposite of after. Baby Animal brushes his teeth **before** going to bed.

bell

bells

A **bell** is for ringing. Baby Fozzie rings the dinner **bell**.

below

Below is the opposite of above. There is a bee **below** the bell.

big

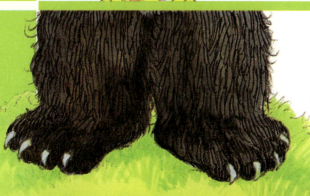

Big means large, not small. This bear is so **big**, we can only see his feet.

bird
birds

A **bird** is an animal with feathers and wings. This **bird** is feeding her babies.

birthday
birthdays

Your **birthday** is the day you were born. People often have parties on their **birthdays**.

black

Black is the darkest color. The big **black** bear sits in a blue boat

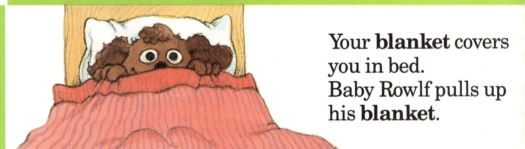

blanket
blankets

Your **blanket** covers you in bed. Baby Rowlf pulls up his **blanket**.

blue

Blue is a color. Baby Gonzo flies his **blue** airplane in the **blue** sky over the **blue** lake.

boat
boats

You travel on water in a **boat**. Baby Kermit rows the **boat**.

body

bodies

A **body** is all the parts of something, including you. Can you name all the parts of your **body**?

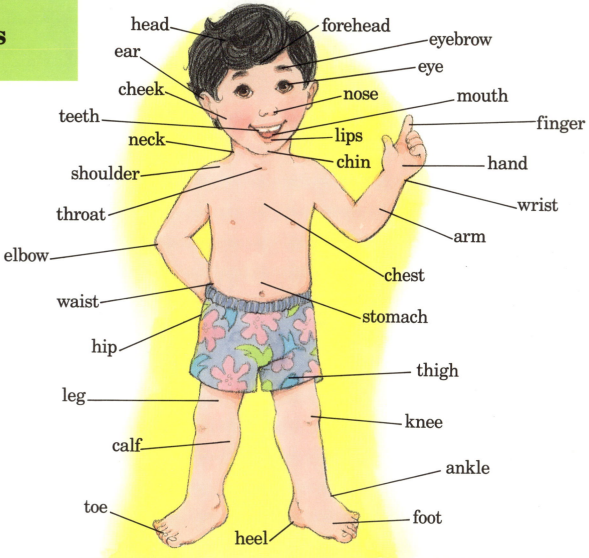

head — forehead — eyebrow — eye
ear — nose — mouth — finger
cheek — lips — hand
teeth — chin — wrist
neck — arm
shoulder — chest
throat — stomach
elbow — thigh
waist — knee
hip — ankle
leg — foot
calf — heel
toe

book

books

A **book** has pages, words, and pictures. **Books** are for reading. The big black bear reads a blue **book**.

boot

boots

A **boot** is a kind of shoe for rain or snow. Baby Scooter puts on his **boot**.

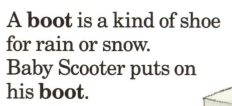

bottle

bottles

A **bottle** is a container that can hold liquids. Baby Kermit pours milk from a **bottle**.

bowl

bowls

A **bowl** is a round dish. Baby Gonzo has cereal in his **bowl**.

box

boxes

A **box** is a container with four sides, a bottom, and sometimes a lid. Baby Scooter's other boot is in the **box**.

boy

boys

A **boy** is a male child. The **boy** throws the ball to the dog.

bread

Bread is a food made with flour and baked in an oven. Baby Piggy puts butter on her **bread**.

breakfast

breakfasts

You eat **breakfast** in the morning. The Muppet Babies are eating **breakfast**.

brother
brothers

Your **brother** is a boy who has the same mother and father as you do. Scooter is Skeeter's **brother**.

brown

Brown is the color of chocolate. Baby Rowlf is **brown**.

brush
brushes

You use a **brush** to keep your hair neat, clean your teeth, or paint. Baby Piggy brushes her hair with a **brush**.

butter

Butter is a yellow food that is made from milk. Baby Fozzie puts **butter** on his corn.

butterfly
butterflies

A **butterfly** is an insect with colorful wings. Three yellow **butterflies** fly in the air.

button
buttons

You keep your clothes closed with **buttons**. Baby Gonzo buttons one **button** at a time.

Cc

cake

cakes

Cake is a sweet, baked dessert. Baby Kermit's birthday **cake** has four candles on it.

car

cars

A **car** has four wheels and an engine. You go places in a **car**. Baby Kermit got a toy **car** for his birthday.

carrot

carrots

A **carrot** is an orange vegetable. **Carrots** grow in the ground.

cat

cats

A **cat** is a small, furry animal that makes a good pet. The **cat** plays with a ball.

catch

catches

To **catch** is to get or grab. Baby Fozzie **catches** the ball.

cave

caves

A **cave** is a big hole in rock or earth. This **cave** is very dark.

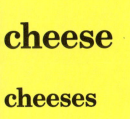

chair

chairs

A **chair** is furniture to sit on. Baby Bunsen sits on a **chair**.

cheese

cheeses

Cheese is a food made from milk. The mouse eats the **cheese**.

chest

chests

A **chest** is a box to keep things in. Also, your **chest** is between your neck and your stomach. Baby Animal wears a bib that covers his **chest**.

chew

chews

You **chew** with your teeth. Baby Animal **chews** on an apple.

chicken

chickens

A **chicken** is a
kind of bird.
This **chicken** lives
on a farm.

child

children

A **child** is a boy or girl.
The **child** helps Statler
cross the street.

chin

chins

Your **chin** is the part of your
face below your mouth.
Baby Bunsen has chocolate
ice cream all over his **chin**.

chocolate

chocolates

Chocolate is a sweet food.
Baby Bunsen likes
chocolate ice cream.

circle

circles

A **circle** is a round
and flat shape.
Baby Rowlf draws a **circle**.

city

cities

A **city** is bigger than a town.
Many people live in a **city**.

clap
claps

To **clap** is to hit your hands together to make a sound. The Muppet Babies **clap** their hands.

clay

You use **clay** to make things. Baby Gonzo makes a chicken from **clay**.

clean
cleans

To **clean** is to tidy up or wash away dirt. The Muppet Babies **clean** the window.

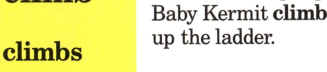

climb
climbs

To **climb** is to go up. Baby Kermit **climbs** up the ladder.

clock
clocks

A **clock** is an instrument that tells time. Baby Rowlf fixes the **clock**.

clothes

Clothes are what you wear on your body. Shirts and skirts are **clothes**.

cloud
clouds

A **cloud** is many small drops of water floating together in the sky. Rain comes from **clouds**.

clown
clowns

Clowns are people who make you laugh. Baby Fozzie pretends to be a **clown**.

coat
coats

A **coat** is something to wear when it is rainy or cold. Baby Rowlf wears his new **coat**.

cold

Cold is the opposite of hot. Kermit and Rowlf like to play outside when it is **cold**.

color
colors

Baby Gonzo is using many **colors** in his picture.

red orange yellow green blue purple violet

comb
combs

A **comb** has long, thin teeth. You use a **comb** to keep your hair neat.
Baby Piggy combs her doll's hair with a **comb**.

come
comes

To **come** is to move toward someone or something.

Please **come** to the table, Baby Animal.

cook
cooks

To **cook** is to prepare food by heating it.
The Swedish Chef **cooks** soup in a pot.

cookie
cookies

A **cookie** is a small, flat cake. Baby Gonzo saves his **cookie** for dessert.

corn

Corn is a vegetable that people and animals eat. Baby Piggy likes to eat **corn**.

count
counts

You **count** to find out how many things there are.
How many cookies can you **count** on this page? (Answer below.)

Answer: There are eight cookies on this page. Did you **count** the cookie near the cookie definition?

Cc

cover

covers

To **cover** is to put one thing over something else. Baby Gonzo **covers** himself with his blanket.

cow

cows

A **cow** is a big animal. Milk comes from **cows.** This **cow** is brown.

crawl

crawls

To **crawl** is to move on hands and knees. Baby Animal **crawls** on the floor.

cry

cries

To **cry** is to sob or weep when you're sad or hurt. Why does Baby Animal **cry**?

cup

cups

A **cup** is a small bowl with a handle. Baby Animal has spilled his **cup** of milk.

cut

cuts

To **cut** is to make pieces out of something. Baby Piggy **cuts** a circle out of paper.

Dd

dad
dads

Dad is another word for father.
This **dad** and his daughter are ice-skating.

dance
dances

To **dance** is to move to music. Baby Piggy loves to **dance** all day.

dark

Dark is when there is little or no light. Baby Piggy goes to bed when it is **dark**.

daughter
daughters

If you are a girl, you are the **daughter** of your mother and father.
Two **daughters** of the same mother and father are sisters.

day
days

Day is when it is light outside. The Muppet Babies play all **day**.

desk
desks

A **desk** is a table with drawers. **Desks** are used for writing. Pirate Kermit finds a map in the **desk.**

dessert
desserts

You sometimes eat **dessert** after lunch or dinner. Fruit makes a good **dessert**.

dictionary
dictionaries

A **dictionary** tells you what words mean. This book is a **dictionary**.

dig
digs

To **dig** is to make a hole in the ground. Pirate Kermit **digs** for gold.

dinner
dinners

Dinner is the biggest meal of the day. The Muppet Babies are eating **dinner**.

dirt

Dirt is mud or earth. Baby Animal is covered with **dirt**.

dish
dishes

A **dish** is a plate that holds food. Baby Piggy carries a **dish**.

dive
dives

To **dive** is to jump headfirst into something, usually water. Baby Gonzo **dives** into the pool.

do
does

When you make something happen, you **do** it. Baby Gonzo **does** a fantastic double flip.

doctor
doctors

A **doctor** takes care of you when you get sick. The **doctor** looks in Baby Piggy's ear.

dog
dogs

A **dog** is a furry animal that barks. Some **dogs** are big; other **dogs** are small.

doll
dolls

A **doll** is a toy that looks like a baby, a child, a man, or a woman.

Baby Piggy's **doll** wears a green dress.

door
doors

A **door** is an opening for going in or out. The **door** is open.

down

To go **down** is to move from a higher place to a lower place. Baby Gonzo goes **down** the stairs.

draw
draws

To **draw** is to make a picture or shape. Baby Gonzo **draws** a picture of Baby Piggy's doll.

drawer
drawers

A **drawer** is a place to keep things. Baby Piggy finds her comb in the **drawer**.

dream
dreams

A **dream** is something you see while you sleep. In Baby Skeeter's **dream**, she flies an airplane.

dress
dresses

Dresses are clothes that women and girls wear. Baby Piggy wears a pink **dress**.

drink
drinks

To **drink** is to swallow liquid. Baby Fozzie **drinks** his milk.

drive
drives

To **drive** is to make something go. Baby Kermit **drives** his car to the store.

drum
drums

A **drum** is an instrument that you hit to make a sound. Baby Animal plays a big **drum**.

dry

Dry is the opposite of wet. To stay **dry**, use an umbrella.

duck
ducks

A **duck** is a web-footed bird that swims. The **duck** likes to get wet.

E e

ear
ears

You hear sounds with your **ears**. Baby Fozzie scratches his **ear**.

early

You are **early** when you do something before most other people do it. Farmers work **early** in the morning.

earth

Earth is ground or dirt. **Earth** is also the planet we live on. Baby Gonzo goes from **earth** to the moon.

easy

Easy means not hard to do. Flying a rocket is **easy** for Baby Gonzo.

eat

eats

To **eat** is to chew and swallow food.
Baby Animal wants to **eat** everything.

egg

eggs

An **egg** can be food. Some baby birds or other animals hatch from **eggs**.
The chicken has an **egg** in her nest.

eight

Eight is the number after seven and before nine.
A spider has **eight** legs.

elbow

elbows

Your **elbow** is where your arm bends.
Baby Piggy wears bracelets up to her **elbow**.

elephant

elephants

An **elephant** is a very big animal.
The **elephant** has a long nose called a trunk.

end

ends

The **end** is the last part of something.
This is the **end** of this page.

engine
engines

An **engine** makes things go.
A car has an **engine**.

erase
erases

To **erase** is to remove.
Baby Gonzo **erases**
his drawing.

explore
explores

To **explore** is to search
or examine.
Baby Kermit **explores**
the cave.

extra

Something you don't need is **extra**.
Baby Piggy has one **extra** sock.

eye
eyes

You look and see
with your **eyes**.
Baby Fozzie is
rubbing his **eye**.

eyebrow
eyebrows

Your **eyebrow** is the line
of hair that grows
above your eye.
Baby Fozzie raises
his **eyebrows**.

F f

face

faces

Eyes, nose, cheeks, forehead, mouth, and chin make a **face**. Baby Piggy looks at her **face** in the mirror.

fall

falls

Fall is the season between summer and winter. Also, to **fall** is to drop down from a higher place. The apple **falls** off the tree.

family

families

A **family** is made up of related people, animals, or things. Some **families** are big; other **families** are small.

far

Far is the opposite of near. Gonzo is **far** away.

farm
farms

A **farm** is a place where people grow plants and raise animals. Baby Gonzo visits the chickens on the **farm**.

fast

Fast means at great speed. It is the opposite of slow. Baby Kermit runs very **fast**.

fat

Fat is the opposite of thin. The **fat** cat ate the cake.

father
fathers

A **father** is a man who has a child. This girl's **father** is a farmer.

feel
feels

To **feel** is to touch something with your hand. Also, you can **feel** happy or sad. Baby Fozzie **feels** happy.

find
finds

To **find** is to discover. Can you **find** the fox in this picture?

finger
fingers

Your **finger** is part of your hand.
How many **fingers** is
Baby Kermit holding up?

fire

Fire is heat and light caused
when something burns.
Statler sits in front of the **fire**.

first

First comes before
anything else.
Baby Piggy is **first**
in line for breakfast.

fish

A **fish** is an animal
that lives in water.
Fish use their fins
to move about.

five

Five is the number after
four and before six.
There are **five** fish
in the fishbowl.

fix
fixes

To **fix** is to make something work
that has been broken.
Baby Animal **fixes** his toy
airplane with glue.

float
floats

To **float** is to rest on the water.
Baby Kermit **floats** on the lake.

floor
floors

The **floor** is what you walk on inside.
Baby Scooter plays on the **floor**.

flour

Flour is used to make some foods.
Bread, cake, and noodles are made from **flour**.

flower
flowers

A **flower** is a plant.
Flowers come in all colors.
Baby Kermit gives Baby Piggy a **flower**.

fly
flies

To **fly** is to move through the air like a bird.
Baby Skeeter **flies** in an airplane.

fold
folds

To **fold** is to bend part of something over the rest of it.
Baby Rowlf **folds** a piece of paper to make a paper airplane.

food
foods

People, animals, and plants need **food** to live. Baby Piggy eats a lot of **food**.

foot
feet

At the end of your leg is your **foot**. Baby Fozzie holds his **foot**.

fork
forks

A **fork** is a tool for picking up things like food. Baby Piggy eats with a **fork**.

four

Four is the number after three and before five. This monster has **four** feet, **four** legs, **four** arms, and **four** eyes.

fox
foxes

A **fox** is a wild animal in the dog family. Is this **fox** in Baby Rowlf's family?

friend
friends

Friends are people whom you like and who also like you. Baby Fozzie is Kermit's **friend**.

Ff

frog
frogs

A **frog** is a small animal that lives both on the ground and in the water. The **frog** hops into the water.

front

Front is the opposite of back. Baby Piggy is at the **front** of the line.

fruit
fruits

Fruit is a sweet food that grows on trees and bushes. There are three kinds of **fruit** in this bowl: apples, grapes, and peaches.

fun

Fun is having a good time. The Muppet Babies are having **fun**.

fur

Fur is the soft hair that covers some animals. Baby Fozzie has **fur**.

G g

game

games

A **game** is something you play. Leapfrog is a **game**.

gift

gifts

A **gift** is something you give to someone. Baby Kermit gives Piggy a birthday **gift**.

giraffe

giraffes

A **giraffe** is an animal with a long neck. The **giraffe** eats leaves for dinner.

girl

girls

A **girl** is a female child. The **girl** feeds the giraffe.

give

gives

Give is the opposite of take. Gonzo **gives** Camilla some grapes.

glass

glasses

A **glass** is something you drink from. Also, **glass** is hard, clear, and easy to break. Windows are usually made of **glass**.

glove

gloves

A **glove** is a mitten with a place for each finger. Baby Piggy pulls on her **gloves**.

glue

Glue is a liquid used to stick things together. Baby Gonzo uses **glue** to make his toy rocket.

go

goes

To **go** is to move from one place to another place. The car **goes** up the hill.

goat

goats

A **goat** is an animal with four legs and two horns. **Goats** like to climb hills

gold

Gold is a yellow metal.
Baby Piggy likes this **gold** ring.

good

Good is the opposite of bad.
Baby Animal is doing a
good job of putting
away his toys.

good-bye

Good-bye is the opposite
of hello.
Baby Kermit waves
good-bye to Baby Fozzie.

grandfather

grandfathers

Your **grandfather** is the father
of your mother or father.
The boy visits his
grandfather and grandmother.

grandmother

grandmothers

Your **grandmother** is the mother
of your father or mother.
The boy's **grandmother**
and grandfather are
happy to see him.

grape

grapes

A **grape** is a fruit that grows in bunches.
Grapes are used to make juice and jelly.

grass

gray

green

ground

grow

grows

guess

guesses

Grass is a green plant that grows in the ground.
Grass grows in the park.

Gray is the color
you get when you
mix black and white.
This rabbit is **gray**.

Green is the color of grass.
Kermit is happy
to be **green**.

The **ground** is
the earth.
The flowers grow
in the **ground**.

To **grow** is to get bigger.
Water and sun help
flowers to **grow**.

When you don't know the answer
to a question, you **guess**.
Guess which hand holds the grapes?

H h

hair
hairs

Hair covers parts of your head and other parts of your body. Beaker has red **hair**.

hammer
hammers

A **hammer** is a tool. The man hammers the nail with a **hammer**.

hand
hands

Your **hands** are at the ends of your wrists. Baby Fozzie waves his **hand**.

handle

You hold something by its **handle**. Baby Animal picks up the cup by its **handle**.

happy

When you are **happy**, you feel good. Baby Piggy is **happy** that Kermit is giving her a gift.

hard

Hard is the opposite of soft. **Hard** is also the opposite of easy. It is **hard** for Baby Animal to tie his shoelaces.

hat

hats

A **hat** covers your head. The horse wears a **hat**.

head

heads

Your **head** is a part of your body. **Head** also means the top of something.

hear

hears

People and animals **hear** sounds with their ears. The horse **hears** the horn.

heart

hearts

The **heart** is a muscle that helps move blood through the body. A **heart** is also a shape.

Hello.

hello

Hello is what you say when you meet someone. Baby Fozzie says **hello** to Baby Kermit.

help
helps

You **help** people or animals when they need you. Baby Kermit **helps** Piggy dig a hole.

hide
hides

To **hide** is to disappear so that no one can find you. One goat **hides** behind a tree.

high

High is the opposite of low. Baby Fozzie is **high** up on the hill.

hill
hills

A **hill** is a mound of earth or sand or rock. There are goats on the **hill**.

hip
hips

Your **hip** is below your waist and above your leg. Simon says: Put your hands on your **hips**.

hit
hits

hold
holds

hole
holes

honey

hood
hoods

hop
hops

To **hit** is to strike something with your hand or with something else. Baby Kermit **hits** the ball.

To **hold** is to carry or grasp. Baby Kermit **holds** the bat.

A **hole** is an opening or a space in something. There is a **hole** in the tree.

Honey is a sweet food that bees make. Baby Piggy puts some **honey** in her basket.

A **hood** covers your head and neck. What color is Baby Piggy's **hood**?

To **hop** is to jump up and down on one foot or both feet. The rabbit **hops** across the road.

Honey

horn
horns

A **horn** is an instrument that you blow into to make a sound. **Horns** also grow on some animals' heads.

horse
horses

A **horse** is an animal with four legs. Cowboy Kermit rides a **horse**.

hot

Hot is the opposite of cold. Fire is too **hot** to touch.

hour
hours

One **hour** is sixty minutes. There are twenty-four **hours** in a day.

house
houses

A **house** is a building that people live in. Why is the horse in the **house**?

hurt
hurts

To **hurt** is to make someone or yourself feel bad. Skeeter **hurt** her knee.

I i

I am Baby Kermit.

I

I is a word you use when you talk about yourself.

ice

Ice is frozen water. Baby Bunsen ice-skates across the ice.

ice cream

Ice cream is a food made from milk. Baby Piggy eats ice cream.

idea

ideas

An idea is something you think of. Baby Bunsen has a good idea! He is using an umbrella to move faster.

in

In is the opposite of out.
The teddy bear is **in** the box.

ink

Ink is a colored liquid
that you use to write
or draw.
Kermit loves to draw
in green **ink**.

insect
insects

An **insect** is a tiny
animal with six legs.
Some **insects** fly;
other **insects** crawl.

inside

Inside means to be
in something.
Baby Kermit is **inside**
the house.

iron
irons

An **iron** is something
used to press clothes.
Iron is also a metal.

itch
itches

An **itch** is a feeling that makes
you want to scratch.
An insect bite often **itches**.

Jj

jacket

jackets

A **jacket** is something you wear to keep warm. Baby Kermit has a new red winter **jacket**.

jar

jars

A **jar** is a container for food or other things. Baby Animal puts the lid on the **jar** of jelly.

jelly

jellies

Jelly is a sweet food made from fruit. Baby Animal makes a peanut butter-and-**jelly** sandwich.

jet

jets

A **jet** is a kind of airplane. The **jet** flies over the ocean.

job
jobs

A **job** is work that you do. Baby Kermit's **job** is to shovel the snow.

join
joins

To **join** is to put two or more things together. Baby Fozzie **joins** his friends.

joke
jokes

A **joke** makes you laugh. Baby Fozzie tells a **joke** to Baby Kermit and Baby Piggy.

juice

Juice is a liquid made by squeezing fruits or vegetables. Baby Animal drinks orange **juice**.

jump
jumps

To **jump** is to lift your feet off the ground at the same time. The cow **jumps** over the moon.

jungle
jungles

A **jungle** is a wild place with plants and animals. Baby Kermit drives through the **jungle**.

K k

kangaroo

kangaroos

A **kangaroo** is a big animal that carries its babies in a pouch on its stomach. The **kangaroo** hops on two strong legs.

keep

keeps

To **keep** is to have something for a long time. Baby Kermit **keeps** the key.

key

keys

A **key** opens or closes a lock. Baby Kermit uses the **key** to unlock the door

kick

kicks

To **kick** is to hit with your foot. Baby Fozzie **kicks** the ball.

kind

To be **kind** is to be nice.
The king is **kind** to
the knight.

king

kings

A **king** is a man who is
the leader of a country.
The **king** wears a
gold crown.

kiss

kisses

To **kiss** is to touch
with the lips.
Baby Piggy **kisses**
Baby Kermit.

kitchen

kitchens

A **kitchen** is a room where
people cook food.
The Swedish Chef cooks
corn in the **kitchen**.

kite

kites

A **kite** is a toy with a long string.
Kites fly in the wind.
Baby Gonzo flies his **kite** at the beach.

kitten

kittens

A **kitten** is a baby cat.
The **kitten** plays with the
string on Baby Gonzo's kite.

knee
knees

Your leg bends at the **knee**. Simon says: Put your hands on your **knees**.

knife
knives

A **knife** is a tool for cutting. **Knives** should always be held by their handles.

knight
knights

A **knight** was a soldier of long ago. **Knights** wore armor and rode horses into battle.

knock
knocks

To **knock** is to hit something to make a sound. It is polite to **knock** before you open a door.

knot
knots

A **knot** is string, rope, or ribbon tied together. Cub Scout Fozzie is learning to tie a **knot**.

know
knows

When you **know** something, you are sure about it. Baby Kermit **knows** how to spell his name.

Ll

lake

lakes

A **lake** is a big body of water. Baby Kermit sails his boat on the **lake**.

lamp

lamps

A **lamp** is something that gives off light. Baby Piggy turns off the **lamp** when she goes to sleep.

laugh

laughs

You **laugh** when something is funny. Baby Gonzo **laughs** at the clown.

leaf

leaves

A **leaf** is a part of a plant. Baby Bunsen collects **leaves** in the fall.

learn

learns

When you **learn** something, you know it. Baby Fozzie **learns** to read.

left

Left is the opposite of right. The ball is on the **left**.

leg

legs

Your **leg** is between your hip and your foot. Simon says: Shake your **leg**!

letter

letters

A **letter** is part of a word. A **letter** is also something you write to someone.

lift

lifts

To **lift** is to pick something up. Baby Kermit **lifts** the apples.

light

Light is the opposite of dark. It is **light** during the day.

like

likes

To **like** is to enjoy someone or something. Baby Kermit **likes** Piggy. He also **likes** apples.

line

lines

A **line** is a long, thin mark. Baby Rowlf writes a letter between the **lines**.

lion

lions

A **lion** is a big, wild animal. You can see **lions** at the zoo.

lip

lips

Lips are the two parts of your face around your mouth. You use your **lips** to smile, talk, and kiss.

liquid

liquids

A **liquid** is wet. Milk and water are **liquids**.

long

Long is the opposite of short. The giraffes have **long** necks.

look

looks

To **look** is to use your eyes to see something. Baby Kermit helps Baby Piggy **look** for her mittens.

lose

loses

If you **lose** something, you can't find it. It is easy to **lose** white mittens in the snow.

loud

Loud is the opposite of quiet or soft. Baby Animal makes a **loud** sound on his drum.

love

loves

To **love** is to like very much. Baby Fozzie **loves** his teddy bear.

low

Low is the opposite of high. Baby Animal's chair is too **low**.

lunch

lunches

You eat **lunch** in the middle of the day. Baby Gonzo eats a pickle-and-cheese sandwich for **lunch**.

Mm

mad

When you are **mad**, you are angry.
Baby Piggy is **mad** that there are no more apples.

make

makes

When you **make** a thing, you have something that wasn't there before.
Baby Gonzo **makes** a mask from paper.

man

men

When a boy grows up, he is a **man**.
This **man** has a son and a daughter.

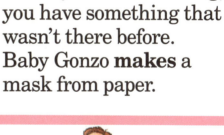

map

maps

A **map** is a picture that shows where something is.
Pirate Kermit's **map** shows where the treasure is.

mask
masks

A **mask** covers your face. Baby Gonzo wears a **mask** on Halloween.

me

Me is a word you use when you talk about yourself.

I'll bet you didn't know **me** with my mask on!

metal
metals

Metal is a hard material used to make things like cars, airplanes, and tools. This pot is made of **metal**.

milk

Milk is a white liquid that many people and animals drink. The **milk** we drink usually comes from cows.

minute
minutes

One **minute** is sixty seconds. There are sixty **minutes** in an hour.

mitten
mittens

A **mitten** covers your hand and keeps it warm. Baby Piggy wears **mittens** when it's cold.

mix

mixes

To **mix** is to stir together. Baby Kermit **mixes** milk, eggs, and flour to make pancakes.

mom

moms

Mom is another word for mother. The child waves to her **mom**.

monkey

monkeys

A **monkey** is an animal with long arms and legs. **Monkeys** like to climb trees.

month

months

One **month** is about four weeks. There are twelve **months** in a year: January, February, March, April, May, June, July, August, September, October, November, and December.

moon

moons

The **moon** is an object that travels around the earth. We often see the **moon** in the sky at night.

morning

mornings

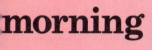

The **morning** is the first part of the day. Baby Kermit wakes up in the **morning**.

mother

mothers

A **mother** is a woman who has a child.
Other words for **mother** are mom and mommy.

mouse

mice

Mice are small animals with long tails. This **mouse** lives in a mouse hole.

mouth

mouths

Your **mouth** is the part of your face that you eat and talk with. Don't talk with your **mouth** full!

move

moves

To **move** is to not stand still. People can also **move** to another house.

mud

When you mix dirt and water, you get **mud**. Baby Animal likes to make **mud** pies.

music

Music is sound formed into pretty patterns. The Muppet Babies are making **music**.

Nn

nail

nails

You have **nails** on your fingers and toes.
A **nail** is also a small piece of metal with a round head on top.
Baby Skeeter hammers the **nail** into the board.

name

names

A **name** is a word for a person, place, or thing.

N, my **name** is Nancy, and my husband's **name** is Nick, and I come from Nebraska, and I sell nuts.

nap

naps

A **nap** is a short sleep that you take during the day.
Baby Animal takes his **nap** when he is sleepy.

near

Near is the opposite of far.
Baby Kermit is **near** the edge of this page.

neck
necks

Your **neck** is between your head and your shoulders.
Baby Bunsen wears a scarf around his **neck.**

nest
nests

A **nest** is the place where birds lay their eggs.
The bird sits in her **nest**.

new

New is the opposite of old.
Baby Piggy is showing off her **new** red shoes.

night
nights

Night is the opposite of day.
At **night**, the Muppet Babies sleep.

nine

Nine is the number after eight and before ten.
Can you count the **nine** nails in this picture?

no

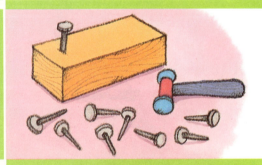

No is the opposite of yes.
No, Baby Animal. Don't draw on this page!

nod
nods

A **nod** is when you move your head up and down. A **nod** usually means yes.
Simon says: **Nod** your head!

noise
noises

A **noise** is a loud sound. Baby Animal likes to make **noise** with pots and pans.

none

None means not any. Baby Skeeter has nine nails; Baby Gonzo has **none**.

noon

Noon is twelve o'clock in the middle of the day. **Noon** is a good time for lunch.

nose
noses

A **nose** is what people and animals smell with. Baby Gonzo's **nose** can almost touch his toes!

note
notes

A **note** is a short letter or message.
Here is a **note** for you.

Dear reader,
Please go on to the next page.
Thank you.

nothing

Nothing means no thing.
This box has **nothing** in it.

now

Now means right this minute.
Baby Animal needs to wash
his hands right **now**.

number

numbers

A **number** tells you how many
of something you have.
The **number** of nuts near
the squirrel is nine.

nurse

nurses

A **nurse** is someone who
takes care of people in
school or in the hospital.
The **nurse** takes care
of Baby Beaker.

nut

nuts

A **nut** is a seed
with a hard shell.
The squirrel is saving
nuts for food in the winter.

O o

oar

oars

An **oar** is used to row a boat. This **boat** has two oars.

ocean

oceans

An **ocean** is the biggest body of water on earth. Fish swim in **oceans**.

off

Off is the opposite of on. The old man's hat falls **off** his head.

old

Old is the opposite of young. It is also the opposite of new. The **old** man lives in an **old** house.

on

On is the opposite of off. There are four oranges **on** the table.

once

Once means at one time. **Once** there was an old woman who lived in a shoe.

one

One is the number after zero and before two. The old man takes **one** orange off the table.

open

opens

You **open** something so that you or something else can get in or out of it. Baby Fozzie **opens** the door.

opposite

opposites

Two things that are completely different from each other are **opposites**. Up is the **opposite** of down.

orange

oranges

Orange is the color you get when you mix red and yellow. An **orange** is also a fruit. The old man eats the **orange orange**.

out

Out is the opposite of in.
Baby Fozzie goes **out** to play.

outside

Outside is the opposite of inside.
Baby Fozzie is **outside**.

oven

ovens

An **oven** is used
to bake food.
The Swedish Chef
bakes a pie
in the **oven**.

over

Over is the opposite of under.
The moon is **over** the cows.

Whoooo!

owl

owls

An **owl** is a bird with
big, round eyes that
sleeps all day.
Owls hoot at night.

P p

page
pages

A **page** is one of the pieces of paper in a book. Please look at each **page** in this book.

pail
pails

A **pail** is a container with a handle. Baby Piggy's **pail** is full of sand.

paint
paints

Paint is a colored liquid that you use to make pictures. Baby Gonzo uses pink **paint** to paint his picture.

pajamas

Pajamas are clothes to sleep in. Baby Fozzie puts on his **pajamas**.

pan
pans

A **pan** is a container for cooking.
The Swedish Chef cooks eggs in a **pan**.

pants

Pants are clothes that cover your legs.
Baby Piggy wears blue **pants**.

paper
papers

Paper is used for writing, drawing, and making books.
This page is made of **paper**.

park
parks

A **park** is a place with plants, grass, and trees that you can visit.
Baby Kermit plays in the **park**.

part
parts

Parts are pieces of the whole.
The Muppet Babies ate **part** of this birthday cake.

party
parties

A **party** is when people get together to have fun.
Baby Piggy is having a birthday **party**.

pea

peas

A **pea** is a green vegetable.
Pass the **peas**, please.

peach

peaches

A **peach** is a sweet,
round summer fruit.
The Swedish Chef picks
peaches for his pie.

pencil

pencils

A **pencil** is a tool for writing
and drawing.
Baby Fozzie draws
with a **pencil**.

people

People are men, women,
and children.
Many **people** live on earth.
You are one of them.

pet

pets

A **pet** is an animal
that lives with people.
Dogs and cats make
good **pets**.

piano

pianos

A **piano** is a musical instrument.
Baby Rowlf plays the **piano**.

picnic

picnics

picture

pictures

pie

pies

pig

pigs

pink

plant

plants

A **picnic** is a party outside with food. The Muppet Babies are having a **picnic**.

A **picture** shows you what someone or something looks like. Baby Gonzo paints a **picture** of a peach.

A **pie** is a baked food with a crust. It is sometimes filled with fruit. The Swedish Chef has baked two peach **pies**.

A **pig** is an animal with short legs and a fat body. This **pig** lives on a farm.

Pink is the color you get when you mix red and white. Baby Piggy wears a **pink** dress.

A **plant** is a living thing that is not an animal. Baby Kermit waters the **plants**.

plate

plates

A **plate** is a dish for food. Baby Gonzo has a lot of food on his **plate**.

play

plays

To **play** is to do something for fun. The Muppet Babies **play** leapfrog in the park.

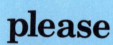

please

Please is the word to use when you ask for something.

Please, Baby Piggy, may I have a peach?

pony

ponies

A **pony** is a small horse. Baby Scooter rides a **pony** in the park.

pool

pools

A **pool** is a small body of water. People swim in swimming **pools**

pot

pots

A **pot** is a container for cooking. The Swedish Chef cooks noodles in a **pot**.

pretend
pretends

To **pretend** is to make believe. Baby Skeeter **pretends** that she's a cowgirl.

pull
pulls

To **pull** is to move something toward you. Baby Gonzo **pulls** his red wagon.

puppy
puppies

A **puppy** is a young dog. The **puppy** sits in the red wagon.

purple

Purple is the color you get when you mix red and blue. These grapes are **purple**.

push
pushes

To **push** is to move something away from you. Baby Skeeter **pushes** a toy truck.

put
puts

To **put** is to place something somewhere. Baby Skeeter **puts** the toy truck in the chest.

Q q

queen
queens

A **queen** is a woman who is the leader of a country. The **queen** wears a silver crown.

question
questions

You ask a **question** when you want to know something. This is a **question**:

> What is your name?

quick

Quick means fast. **Quick**—ask Baby Piggy a question!

quiet

Quiet is when there is no noise. A library is a **quiet** place.

R r

rabbit
rabbits

A **rabbit** is a small, furry animal with long ears. **Rabbits** are sometimes called bunnies.

race
races

A **race** is a contest to see who is the fastest. The rabbit has won the **race.**

rain
rains

Rain is water that falls to the earth from the clouds. Baby Skeeter likes to play in the **rain.**

reach
reaches

To **reach** is to be able to touch something. Now Baby Animal can **reach** the toy truck.

read
reads

To **read** is to understand words on a page or a sign. Can you **read** this book?

rectangle
rectangles

A **rectangle** is a four-sided shape. Baby Rowlf draws a **rectangle.**

red

Red is a bright color. This fire truck is **red.**

ride
rides

To **ride** is to move in or on something. Baby Kermit **rides** on the train.

right

Right is the opposite of left. **Right** is also the opposite of wrong. The blue ball is on the **right.** That's **right!**

ring
rings

When you **ring** a bell, it makes a sound. Also, a **ring** is something you wear on your finger. This girl has **rings** on her fingers.

Rr

river
rivers

A **river** is a body of water that flows to the ocean. Baby Gonzo sees the boats sail down the **river.**

road
roads

A **road** is a path for people, cars, and trucks. This is the **road** to the barn.

rock
rocks

A **rock** is a big stone. Baby Skeeter found a pretty **rock** in the park.

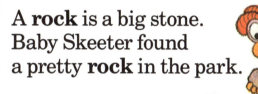

rocket
rockets

A **rocket** travels into outer space. This **rocket** is going to the stars.

roof
roofs

A **roof** is the cover for a building. The rain falls on the **roof.**

room
rooms

A **room** is inside a building. The kitchen is the **room** where you cook dinner.

rose
roses

A **rose** is a flower that smells good. Baby Piggy has a red **rose.**

round

Round is the shape of a ball. The earth is also **round.**

row
rows

A **row** is a straight line of things.
Also, to **row** is to pull a boat through the water with oars. Baby Kermit **rows** the boat.

rug
rugs

A **rug** covers the floor. The big bear sits on the red **rug.**

ruler
rulers

A **ruler** is used to measure things. Baby Scooter measures the insect with a **ruler.**

run
runs

To **run** is to move your feet very fast. Baby Piggy **runs** down the road.

S s

sad

Sad is the opposite of happy.
Baby Fozzie is **sad** because he has lost his teddy bear.

salt

Salt looks like white sand. We put **salt** on our food to make it taste good.
The water in the ocean has **salt** in it.

sand

Sand is tiny bits of rock you find on the beach.
Baby Fozzie's teddy bear is under the **sand.**

school

schools

School is a place where you learn and have fun, too.
Baby Kermit will learn to read in **school.**

scratch
scratches

To **scratch** is to rub something sharp against something else. To **scratch** also means to rub something that itches.

sea
seas

The **sea** is a big body of water. Pirate Kermit sails the **sea** in his ship.

season
seasons

A **season** is part of a year. Each **season** is three months long. The four **seasons** are: winter, spring, summer, and fall.

second
seconds

One **second** is a very short time. There are sixty **seconds** in a minute.

see
sees

To **see** is to use your eyes. **See** Gonzo run.

seed
seeds

A **seed** is the part of a plant that grows into a new plant. Baby Bunsen plants some **seeds**.

seven

Seven is the number after six and before eight. Baby Bunsen has planted **seven** seeds.

shape
shapes

Shape is the outside form of something. There are many different **shapes.**

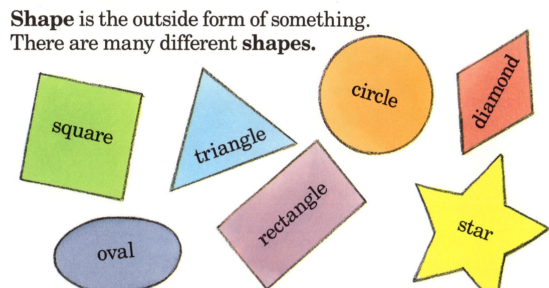

square

triangle

circle

diamond

heart

oval

rectangle

star

sheep

Sheep are gentle animals. A **sheep**'s fur is called wool. Six **sheep** stand in the snow.

shell
shells

A **shell** is a hard covering. A turtle has a **shell.** So does an egg.

ship
ships

A **ship** is a big boat. Pirate Kermit's **ship** sails the seven seas.

shirt

shirts

Shirts are clothes that cover your chest and back.
Baby Fozzie puts on his **shirt.**

shoe

shoes

A **shoe** covers your foot.
How many **shoes** can you wear at one time?

short

Short is the opposite of long.
It is also the opposite of tall.
Baby Kermit is too **short** to reach his book.

shoulder

shoulders

Your **shoulders** are between your neck and your arms.
Simon says: Touch your **shoulders!**

sick

When you do not feel well, you are **sick.**
When Baby Piggy is **sick,** the doctor takes care of her.

sign

signs

A **sign** tells you things in words or pictures.
If you saw these **signs,** what would you do?

silver

Silver is a shiny metal. The queen's crown is made of **silver.**

sing

sings

To **sing** is to make music with your voice. Baby Rowlf **sings** and plays the piano.

sink

sinks

A **sink** is a bowl used for washing. Baby Piggy washes her hands at the **sink.**

sister

sisters

Your **sister** is a girl who has the same mother and father as you do. Skeeter is Scooter's **sister.**

sit

sits

To **sit** is to rest on your bottom. Simon says: **Sit** down on the chair.

six

Six is the number after five and before seven. There are **six** shoes on the rug.

skate

skates

To **skate** is to move with special shoes on your feet. The Muppet Babies **skate** down the road.

skin

skins

Skin is the outside covering on people and animals. Baby Kermit's **skin** is green

skirt

skirts

A **skirt** is a piece of clothing that hangs down from the waist. Baby Skeeter wears a **skirt.**

sky

skies

The **sky** is above the earth. Baby Gonzo sees the birds fly in the blue **sky.**

sleep

sleeps

To **sleep** is to rest with your eyes closed. Baby Gonzo dreams about sheep when he **sleeps.**

slow

Slow is the opposite of fast. The turtle is a **slow** animal.

small

Small is the opposite of big.
The mouse is **small**;
the elephant is big.

smell

smells

You **smell** with your nose.
Baby Piggy **smells** the rose.

smile

smiles

You **smile** with your mouth
when you are happy.
Baby Kermit **smiles** at Piggy.

snake

snakes

A **snake** is a long, thin animal
with no arms or legs.
The **snake** lies in the sun.

sneeze

sneezes

To **sneeze** is to blow out air
suddenly through your
nose and mouth.
Baby Gonzo **sneezes.**

snow

Snow is white ice flakes
that fall from the sky.
Baby Kermit makes
a snowman out of **snow.**

soap

soaps

Soap is used to clean things. Baby Gonzo washes with **soap** and water.

sock

socks

A **sock** is a soft covering for the foot. Baby Scooter takes off his **sock.**

soft

Soft is the opposite of loud. **Soft** is also the opposite of hard. This pillow is **soft.**

son

sons

If you are a boy, you are the **son** of your mother and father. The **son** and daughter of the same mother and father are brother and sister.

sound

sounds

A **sound** is something you hear. Baby Fozzie hears the **sound** of the dinner bell.

soup

soups

Soup is a food made with water or milk. Some **soups** have vegetables in them.

spell
spells

To **spell** is to arrange letters to make words. How do you **spell** "spell"?

spider
spiders

A **spider** is small and has eight legs. **Spiders** use their webs to catch insects to eat.

spoon
spoons

A **spoon** is for eating and mixing. It is easy to eat soup with a **spoon.**

spring
springs

Spring is the season between winter and summer. Flowers grow in the **spring.**

square
squares

A **square** is a shape that has four sides that are the same length. Baby Kermit's book is a **square.**

squirrel
squirrels

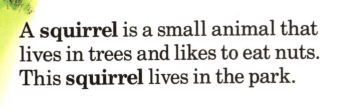

A **squirrel** is a small animal that lives in trees and likes to eat nuts. This **squirrel** lives in the park.

stand

stands

To **stand** is to be up on your feet.
Simon says: **Stand** up.

star

stars

A **star** is a bright object far out in space.
At night, you can sometimes see the **stars**.

step

steps

Steps are stairs.
Also, to **step** is to move one foot.
Baby Rowlf **steps** over the stick.

stick

sticks

A **stick** is a long,
thin piece of wood.
Also, glue helps things
stick together.

stomach

stomachs

Your **stomach** is between
your waist and your legs.
Simon says: Put your hands
on your **stomach.**

stop

stops

Stop is the opposite of go.
Baby Kermit holds the
sign that says **stop.**

store

stores

A **store** is a place where you buy things. Baby Skeeter buys her shoes in a **store.**

story

stories

A **story** tells about something happening. Some **stories** are made up, but others are true. The father reads a **story** to his son.

street

streets

A **street** is a road in a city or town. There are stores on this **street.**

string

strings

String is thin cord or thread. **String** can tie things together or hold beads. Baby Kermit holds the **string** at the end of his kite.

sugar

Sugar makes food taste sweet. Brush your teeth after eating foods with **sugar.**

summer

summers

Summer is the season between spring and fall. The Muppet Babies go to the beach in the **summer.**

sun

The **sun** is a star. It gives the earth light and heat. The earth moves slowly around the **sun.**

swan

swans

A **swan** is a bird with a long neck. Most **swans** are white.

sweater

sweaters

A **sweater** covers the top part of your body and keeps you warm. Baby Scooter wears a blue **sweater.**

sweet

Sugar and honey make food taste **sweet.** Ice cream is a **sweet** dessert.

swim

swims

To **swim** is to move through the water. Frogs like to **swim.**

swing

swings

A **swing** is something you sit on that moves back and forth. Baby Piggy swings on a **swing** in the park.

T t

table
tables

A **table** is furniture to eat at and work at. The Muppet Babies eat lunch at the **table.**

tail
tails

A **tail** is a part of an animal's body. The dog has a white **tail.**

take
takes

Take is the opposite of give. Baby Gonzo **takes** a carrot from Kermit.

talk
talks

Go bye-bye!

To **talk** is to say words. Baby Animal is learning to **talk.**

tall

Tall is the opposite of short. This woman is very **tall.**

taste
tastes

To **taste** is to try a little bit of something. The Swedish Chef **tastes** the soup.

ten

Ten is the number after nine. The tall woman has **ten** toes.

thin

Thin is skinny or narrow. The tall woman is also **thin**

three

Three is the number after two and before four. **Three** Muppet Babies stand in a row.

throw
throws

To **throw** is to use your arm to send something through the air. Baby Scooter **throws** a ball to Baby Skeeter.

thumb
thumbs

Your **thumb** is one of the five fingers on your hand. This is Kermit's **thumb.**

tie
ties

To **tie** is to make a bow or a knot. The strings that you **tie** your shoes with are called shoelaces.

time

Time is yesterday, today, and tomorrow. Minutes, hours, and days are all parts of **time.**

today

Today is the day that it is right now. **Today** you are reading this dictionary.

toe
toes

You have five **toes** on each of your feet. The tall, thin woman touches her **toes.**

tomorrow

Tomorrow is the day after today. If today is Monday, then **tomorrow** is Tuesday.

tongue

tongues

Your **tongue** is inside your mouth. Baby Animal tastes the ice cream with his **tongue.**

tool

tools

A **tool** helps you to do a job. A hammer is a **tool** for hitting nails.

tooth

teeth

Your **teeth** are in your mouth. **Teeth** are for biting and chewing. Baby Animal has a new **tooth.**

touch

touches

To **touch** is to tap very lightly with your hand. Simon says: **Touch** your toes.

town

towns

A **town** is a place where people live. **Towns** are smaller than cities.

toy

toys

A **toy** is something you play with. Baby Gonzo's train is a **toy.**

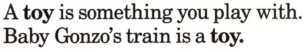

train
trains

A **train** has wheels and an engine. You ride on a **train**. All aboard the **train**!

tree
trees

A **tree** is a large plant. Some **trees** lose their leaves in the fall.

triangle
triangles

A **triangle** is a shape with three sides. Baby Animal draws a **triangle.**

truck
trucks

A **truck** is a large car with wheels and an engine. This **truck** carries trees.

turtle
turtles

A **turtle** is an animal with a hard shell. The **turtles** swim in the water.

two

Two is the number after one and before three. Baby Piggy has **two** arms, **two** legs, **two** ears, and **two** eyes.

U u

umbrella
umbrellas

An **umbrella** keeps you dry in the rain. Baby Kermit holds an **umbrella.**

uncle
uncles

Your **uncle** is the brother of your mother or father. The child of your **uncle** and aunt is your cousin.

under

Under is the opposite of over.
Baby Animal hides **under** the bed.

understand
understands

When you **understand** something, you know it or have a clear idea of it. Baby Kermit **understands** that two comes after one and before three.

undress

undresses

To **undress** means to take off your clothes. Baby Animal **undresses** before he takes his bath.

unhappy

Unhappy means not happy. Baby Animal is **unhappy** because he can't find his rubber duck.

up

Up is the opposite of down. Baby Kermit goes **up** the stairs.

use

uses

To **use** is to put into action. The man **uses** a hammer to build a doghouse.

Vv

vacation
vacations

A **vacation** is time away from work or school. Some people go to the beach on their **vacation.**

van
vans

A **van** is a kind of truck. When families move from one house to another house, they use a moving **van.**

vase
vases

A **vase** is a container for flowers. There are red roses in this **vase.**

vegetable
vegetables

A **vegetable** is a kind of food. Peas, carrots, and beans are all **vegetables.**

very

Very means more than or a lot. The van on the left is big, but the van on the right is **very** big.

view

views

A **view** is what you can see from somewhere. This window has a **view** of the ocean.

visit

visits

To **visit** is to go to see someone or someplace. The brother and sister **visit** their uncle.

voice

voices

Your **voice** is the sound that comes out of your mouth. You sing and talk with your **voice.**

vote

votes

To **vote** is to say if you like something or not. The Muppet Babies **vote** for their favorite game.

Ww

wagon

wagons

A **wagon** has four wheels and is used to carry things. Baby Kermit pulls his blocks in the red **wagon.**

waist

waists

Your **waist** is between your chest and your stomach. Simon says: Put your hands on your **waist.**

walk

walks

To **walk** is to go by moving your feet forward. Baby Rowlf **walks** across the floor.

wall

walls

A **wall** is the side of a room or house. Baby Animal draws on the **wall.**

want
wants

To **want** something means you would like to have it. Baby Piggy **wants** a glass of water.

warm

Warm is between hot and cold. Baby Fozzie is **warm** under his blanket.

wash
washes

To **wash** is to make something clean. Baby Animal **washes** the wall.

water

Water is a clear liquid. Lakes, rivers, oceans, and rain are made of water. Plants, animals, and people need **water** to live.

wave
waves

When water goes up and down, it is called a **wave**. To **wave** is also to move your hand. Baby Gonzo **waves** good-bye.

wear
wears

To **wear** is to put something on. You can **wear** a sweater or a smile.

week

weeks

A **week** is seven days.
They are: Sunday, Monday,
Tuesday, Wednesday, Thursday,
Friday, and Saturday.

well

A **well** is a big hole with
water at the bottom.
Also, **well** is the opposite of sick.
Baby Kermit felt sick this
morning, but now he feels **well.**

wet

Wet is the opposite of dry.
Water is **wet.**

whale

whales

A **whale** is a big animal that lives in the ocean.
Pirate Kermit sees **whales** from his boat.

what

What is a word that often
asks a question.
What is that big animal
swimming in the water?

wheel

wheels

A **wheel** is something round
that helps make things move.
Trains, bicycles, tricyles, and
wagons have **wheels.**

when

When is a word that tells something about time. We will go outside **when** it stops raining.

where

Where is a word that tells something about place. **Where** does the butterfly go when it rains?

white

White is when there is no color at all. The **white** bear walks in the **white** snow.

who

Who is a word for a person. **Who** is wearing the mask?

whole

The **whole** is all of something. Baby Animal ate the **whole** pie.

why

Why is a word that asks for what reason. **Why** is Baby Gonzo wearing a mask?

wild

Wild animals don't usually live with people. This lion is **wild.**

wind

winds

Wind is air that moves. The **wind** blows the leaves off the trees.

window

windows

A **window** is an opening covered with glass. This house has five **windows.**

wing

wings

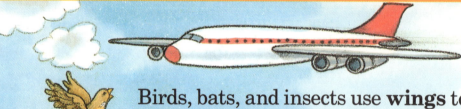

Birds, bats, and insects use **wings** to fly. Airplanes have **wings,** too.

winter

winters

Winter is the season between fall and spring. In many places, it is cold in the **winter.**

wish

wishes

To **wish** for something is to want it very much. Baby Piggy **wishes** for a sunny day.

woman

women

When a girl grows up, she is a **woman.**
These **women** were once little girls.

wood

Wood comes from trees.
Some people build houses
out of **wood.**

word

words

A **word** is made of letters and has a meaning.
You are reading **words** right now.

work

works

To **work** is to do something
that has to be done.
People often **work** to make
money to live.

write

writes

To **write** is to put words on paper.
Baby Piggy **writes** a letter
to Baby Kermit.

wrong

Wrong is the opposite of right.
This is the **wrong** answer.

X x Y y

X ray
X rays

An **X ray** is a picture that shows the inside of something. This is an **X ray** of a tooth.

xylophone
xylophones

A **xylophone** is a musical instrument that you hit to make sounds. Baby Rowlf plays the **xylophone**.

yard
yards

A **yard** is the ground around a house. Baby Piggy grows flowers in her **yard.**

yawn
yawns

When you are sleepy, you open your mouth to **yawn.** Baby Animal **yawns** before his nap.

year
years

A **year** is a long time. There are twelve months in a **year.** Your birthday comes once every **year**.

yellow

Yellow is the color of the sun. Baby Piggy has some **yellow** flowers.

yes

Yes is the opposite of no.

Yes, Baby Piggy. I would like some flowers.

yesterday

Yesterday is the day before today. Was **yesterday** a rainy day or a sunny day?

young

Young is the opposite of old. A child is a **young** person.

yo-yo
yo-yos

A **yo-yo** is a toy that goes up and down on a string. The child plays with a **yo-yo.**

Zz

zebra

zebras

A **zebra** is a black-and-white animal with four legs. A **zebra** looks like a horse with pajamas on.

zero

Zero means none or nothing. **Zero** comes before one. If you have **zero** zebras, you have no zebras.

zipper

zippers

A **zipper** is used to open and close things. Baby Gonzo zips his **zipper.**

zoo

zoos

A **zoo** is a place where people come to see wild animals. The Muppet Babies visit the zebras at the **zoo.**

Aa Bb  Cc

butterfly

Gg giraffe Hh Ii

mouse Mm Nn nod

Rr rock Ss Tt

Ww  xylophone Xx